Routledge Revivals

The British Banking Mechanism

First published in 1951, *The British Banking Mechanism* seeks to enable the reader to obtain a real understanding of the British financial system as it operated back in the 1950s.The book shows how the traditional concept of the Bank of England as the supreme monetary authority controlling the volume of credit has to be modified now that the government, instead of private industry, is the chief borrower from the banking system. This book is of historical importance for scholars and students of banking history, British banking and British economics.

The British Banking Mechanism

W. Manning Dacey

Routledge
Taylor & Francis Group

First published in 1951
by Hutchinson & Co Ltd.

This edition first published in 2025 by Routledge
4 Park Square, Milton Park, Abingdon, Oxon, OX14 4RN

and by Routledge
605 Third Avenue, New York, NY 10017

Routledge is an imprint of the Taylor & Francis Group, an informa business

A Library of Congress record exists under LCCN: 52009980

ISBN: 978-1-032-97740-9 (hbk)
ISBN: 978-1-003-59518-2 (ebk)
ISBN: 978-1-032-97741-6 (pbk)

Book DOI 10.4324/9781003595182

THE BRITISH BANKING MECHANISM

W. Manning Dacey
late Honorary Fellow of
the London School of Economics
Economic Adviser, Lloyds Bank

HUTCHINSON UNIVERSITY LIBRARY
LONDON

HUTCHINSON & CO (*Publishers*) LTD
178–202 Great Portland Street, London W1

London Melbourne Sydney
Auckland Bombay Toronto
Johannesburg New York

★

First published 1951
Reprinted 1952
Second (revised) edition 1958
Third (revised) edition 1960
Fourth (revised) edition 1962
Fifth (revised) edition 1964
Reprinted 1967

The gold bar on the cover of the paperback edition is by courtesy of Johnson, Matthey & Co Ltd

This book has been set in Imprint, printed in Great Britain on Smooth Wove paper by Anchor Press, and bound by Wm. Brendon, both of Tiptree, Essex

CONTENTS

FOREWORD

THIS book, as was stated in the original foreword, seeks to explain the principles which underlie the workings of our banking system as it has existed since 1931.

When the book appeared, on the eve of the return to monetary policy in 1951, Bank Rate had for nineteen years (with the exception of a few weeks at the outbreak of war) been left unchanged at 2 per cent; by contrast, we have to go back as far as 1873 to find a higher peacetime Rate than the 7 per cent imposed in 1957 and again in 1961.

Among the major themes of the original work were the extent to which the central bank's control of the monetary situation is conditioned by government borrowings in the form of floating debt and the importance of the liquidity ratio of commercial banks. Both have been underlined by recent events.

Chapter XVI, written for the revised edition towards the end of 1957, discussed how it was that, six years after the return to monetary policy, inflation still continued and sterling was passing through yet another crisis. It was suggested that September 1957 might conceivably prove to have been 'the turning point in the rake's progress' but that only time could show whether the levelling off of prices represented merely a lull in inflation or the beginning of a new period of monetary stability. Unfortunately, inflationary trends were allowed to reassert themselves and 1961 brought yet another crisis fully as severe as that of 1957. This is the more lamentable as the surplus liquid assets resulting from wartime deficits and the Dalton cheap money policy had been finally absorbed by the process of inflation itself, and by 1957 the stock of money was no longer manifestly excessive. On this occasion, it is suggested in the new final chapter, the harm was done by the failure, in the weak budget of 1960, to match rising expenditure with additional taxation, so that fiscal policy was undermining instead of reinforcing monetary policy.

I am much indebted to my secretary and to other colleagues in Lloyds Bank for their help with the revision. The views expressed of course commit nobody but myself.

W. M. D.
February 1962

CHAPTER 1

SOME FUNDAMENTALS OF DEPOSIT BANKING

FOR our purposes, it will normally be sufficiently near to the truth to think of the stock of money in present-day Britain as consisting of two parts: Bank of England notes and clearing bank deposits. The facts are, of course, more complicated. For small transactions we use, in addition to notes, coin of various denominations, while in some parts of the United Kingdom notes other than those of the Bank of England remain in circulation, notably those issued by the Scottish banks. That itself is a reminder that the London clearing banks do not make up the whole of our system. But the fact that other banking institutions exist does not give rise to any important monetary problems and can easily be fitted into the general picture at a later stage.

One could wax metaphysical about the nature of money, but for our purposes, again, it will be sufficient to define money as anything which is widely accepted in settlement of debts. Important consequences, however, flow from the fact that Bank of England notes and other forms of cash are legal tender money while clearing bank deposits are not: that is to say, a person to whom money is due is not bound to accept a cheque in settlement but is entitled to demand cash.[1] Payment by cheque may sometimes require the creditor to accept a certain degree of risk: for example, in casual transactions, such as payment for a taxi or an isolated purchase at a shop where the debtor is not known to the creditor. But even when the credit-

1. If the creditor refuses an offer of legal tender the debt is not extinguished, but the debtor will have fulfilled his duty of seeking out the creditor to effect payment; the onus – and expense – of collecting the debt then fall upon the creditor.

worthiness of the drawer does not come in question, payment in cash may be more convenient to one or other of the parties – for wage payments in most cases, or for very small purchases.

Where the creditor is willing to accept payment by cheque (and that applies, of course, to the vast bulk of the country's transactions), then the credit balance which is transferred from the account of the drawer of the cheque to that of the payee is 'performing money work' – acting as a medium of exchange – just as efficiently as actual cash. But the creditor is entitled to demand cash in all cases and likely to do so in some. Hence, it is obviously vital to the owner of a bank deposit that his balance should at all times be convertible into cash on demand. The primary duty of any bank is therefore always to maintain a cash reserve sufficient to meet any demands that its customers may make upon it.

One way to be certain of meeting that obligation would be for the bank to hold coin and Bank of England notes equivalent to the whole of its deposit liabilities; in other words, to invest the whole of its assets in cash. In that event, however, the bank would not be earning any income from its assets and would have to recoup the expenses of administering its customers' accounts from some other source, such as specific charges for collecting cheques and for all other services. That is one feasible solution, but it would produce a very different monetary system from the British system we are proposing to describe.

In such a system of pure 'cloakroom' banking, to use Edwin Cannan's expressive phrase,[1] the emergence of the banking habit would not increase the stock of money by a penny, since bank deposits could come into existence only by the withdrawal from circulation and the complete immobilization of an exactly equivalent amount of cash. And the banking habit itself would necessarily be circumscribed, since the depositors would have to bear the full cost of maintaining the banking system. The public would still find it worth while to hold some part of its liquid assets in the form of bank deposits, owing to the risks of loss or theft involved in holding large quantities of notes, the risk and inconvenience of making large payments in notes, the advantage

1. Without in the least accepting Cannan's view that the actual British system is of that nature.

of a bank account as a record of transactions, and so on. But these various conveniences of possessing a bank account would cost the depositor a great deal more than under the present system in which, if he holds a sufficiently large balance, these services and other benefits cost him nothing at all, other than the sacrifice of the interest he might have earned on the money by investing it in some less liquid form.[1]

This cheapness of banking services is directly due to the fact that under the present system the banks themselves do not follow the safety-first rule to the extent of investing the whole of their assets in cash. On the contrary, they find that in practice they can meet all demands for cash made upon them while holding only a very small proportion of their assets in the form of cash. The remainder they invest in various claims to receive cash at some future time, which at this stage we can describe generically as 'securities'. They are in fact partly securities in the ordinary sense, such as short-dated Government bonds; but the term will serve to cover also advances to business firms and other private customers – that is, loans and overdrafts. On these deferred claims to cash, the banks, like any other investors, receive income in the form of interest or dividends. If all goes well, part of these asset earnings will contribute to the banks' profits; the bulk goes to defray the cost of maintaining the organization and providing services to customers either free of specific charges or at less than their true cost.

Consequences vastly more far-reaching than a lowering of the cost of banking services to the depositor flow from this practice of investing bank assets in forms other than cash. The smaller the cash reserve the higher the bank's asset earnings will be, but the less the certainty of its being able to meet demands for cash at a moment's notice. Hence, from the point of view of the bank, a constant tug-of-war between the competing aims of liquidity and profitability. The conflict is resolved in practice by the maintenance of a well-defined conventional assets structure, which varies little from one joint stock bank

1. Since October 1945 the London clearing banks have paid no interest on 'current' accounts; the rate on 'deposit' accounts (i.e., where the customer has agreed to give a period of notice, at present seven days, before withdrawing the funds) is normally 2 per cent under Bank Rate.

to another and is usually fairly stable over long periods. Secondly, this division of bank assets between cash and 'securities' introduces the element of pyramiding, which is a basic feature of the British and, indeed, of all other developed banking systems.

It means that the emergence of the banking habit will tend greatly to increase the stock of money, since the creation of a bank deposit no longer involves the withdrawal from circulation of anything like an equivalent volume of cash. Instead of merely replacing notes pound for pound, in other words, bank deposits will now represent for the most part a net addition to the stock of money. Indeed, if only a very small proportion of bank assets are held in the form of cash, and if the banking habit is widespread, bank deposits will make up by far the greater part of the total money stock.[1]

Moreover, the proportion of bank assets held in the form of cash is very stable – a great deal of banking practice is in fact now based upon the attempt to maintain an absolutely constant cash ratio. This means that *if* the authority controlling the note issue can expand or contract the volume of cash available as bank cash reserves, it can sooner or later bring about a much larger variation in the amount of bank deposits and therefore in the total stock of money.[2] Finally, the practice of investing some part of bank assets in advances to industry and in long-term securities gives the banks a far more significant rôle in the national economy than could ever be the case under mere cloakroom banking.

1. Recent figures for this country are given on p. 22. See also Chapter XVI.

2. Whether that is possible depends, however, as will be shown later, on the supply of other assets which can be turned into bank cash, including (and especially) Treasury bills.

CHAPTER II

THE PYRAMID OF CREDIT

I

ONE of the most confusing things for the beginner is to learn that under modern conditions the principal kinds of money – which we have defined as anything widely accepted in settlement of debts – themselves consist of debts or acknowledgment of debt. That is, of course, true both of bank deposits, which are the banks' debts to their customers, and of bank notes, which embody the issuing bank's promise to 'pay bearer on demand'. If this is confusing, it nevertheless has the advantage that it disposes straight away of any mistaken idea that the value of money – *as* money – derives from any intrinsic value it may possess as a commodity (e.g., a gold coin), and focuses attention on the fundamental characteristic of acceptability.[1]

No confusion need arise if we bear firmly in mind the principle which underlies all double-entry book-keeping: namely, that one man's liability is another man's asset. If you lend me half-a-crown, then I acquire an asset, the half-crown, together with an equal and opposite liability, to repay you the half-crown; so that my books are balanced and my 'net worth', as the Americans call it, is unchanged. You, on the other hand, have exchanged one asset, the half-crown, for a different asset, namely, my undertaking to repay the half-crown. If the loan was well-advised, then the asset which you have acquired (i.e., my liability to repay), will be worth exactly half-a-crown. However, the original half-crown represented cash in hand, whereas my promise to repay relates to a future time, and there is always

1. Subsidiary coins, of course, have some commodity value, but this is less than their monetary value. From the monetary point of view token coins may most usefully be thought of as 'notes stamped on metal'; and it is helpful to think of notes, as Professor Sayers suggests, as a page torn out of a bank's ledger and passed from hand to hand.

the possibility that I may be run over by a bus before the promise is fulfilled; so you are out of your money for a time and are not absolutely certain of coming into it again. Hence the transaction involves you in a sacrifice of liquidity and an element of uncertainty which, if this were a commercial deal and not just a little temporary accommodation between friends, would justify your charging interest on the loan.

Let us make use of this elementary concept to see what would happen if a commercial banking system (and a discount market) were suddenly to spring into existence in a community whose only money had hitherto consisted of notes issued by a government or central bank. From the realistic viewpoint, of course, this illustration does not hold water for a moment. To suppose that a community without commercial banks could possess a central bank is rather like conceiving of an amoeba with a nervous system; nor is the banking habit an overnight growth. But we are concerned at present only with principles, not with empirical realism or historical accuracy.

We will suppose that on the day our bank is established the public pay in £800,000 in notes. The position of the bank is then comparable in kind to mine after the loan of half-a-crown. Its balance sheet, a simple document, would appear as follows:

Liabilities	£	*Assets*	£
Deposits	800,000	Cash in hand	800,000
Total	800,000	Total	800,000

On the following day the bank starts activities. It lends £100,000 to the discount market repayable on demand; uses £100,000 to buy three-months Treasury bills from the Government, which takes payment in cash; and it lends £500,000 to commercial firms who promptly draw out the entire advance in notes, which are used for the payment of wages. This leaves the bank with £100,000 in cash, and its balance sheet now reads:

Liabilities	£	*Assets*	£
Deposits	800,000	Cash in hand	100,000
		Money at call ..	100,000
		Discounts (Treasury bills)	100,000
		Loans and overdrafts	500,000
Total	800,000	Total	800,000

On the third day the bank carries out one more operation. It buys £200,000 of short-dated Government bonds from members of the public who do not draw out the proceeds in cash, but prefer to leave them on deposit with the bank. This is not an unrealistic assumption. The sellers of the securities are admittedly parting with an interest-bearing asset in exchange for one that yields at best a smallish return and may even involve them in payment of bank charges. But they may well regard the convenience of holding some part of their assets in cash or its equivalent – which, unlike the securities, is not exposed to the risk of fluctuations in capital value – as adequate compensation for the sacrifice of interest; in the same way that, as we have already seen, the greater convenience of holding a bank deposit instead of notes may make it worth while not only to forgo interest but even to make some payment to the bank for holding the funds.

Our object in assuming that the funds are left with the bank is to demonstrate that a bank deposit can come into existence without the prior deposit of *cash*. If the seller of an asset is prepared to leave the proceeds on deposit with the bank, and does not use the money to repay an advance previously granted by the bank, then the acquisition by the bank of that asset, whether it be cash or 'securities', will clearly bring an equal and simultaneous increase in the bank's liabilities. This is, of course, the essence of the pyramiding process. For the moment let us take the principle for granted and return instead to the bank's balance sheet, which now takes the following form:

Liabilities	£	*Assets*	£
Deposits	1,000,000	Cash in hand	100,000
		Money at call ..	100,000
		Discounts (Treasury bills)	100,000
		Investments (Government bonds) ..	200,000
		Loans and overdrafts	500,000
Total	1,000,000	Total	1,000,000

In its brief life of three days, in other words, our hypothetical bank will have arrived at a position almost exactly resembling that of the London clearing banks in the years before 1939. It has a cash reserve equal to 10 per cent of its deposits. A further 20 per cent of its assets are invested in bills and call money, making a total of 30 per cent in the three so-called 'liquid assets'. The remaining 70 per cent comprise investments and advances, the two main 'earning assets,' loans and overdrafts to customers accounting for a full half of its assets as a whole.

We will leave to a later stage[1] any discussion of the important implications for banking policy and practice of this conventional assets structure, and its abrupt transformation by the exigencies of deficit finance during the war years. Nor will we spare more than a glance at the facts that this remarkable institution appears to possess neither premises nor a penny of capital of its own, to say nothing of any reserves. Instead, let us look a little more closely at our bank's cash reserve in order to complete our picture of the pyramid of credit. We have already seen that the deposit *liabilities* of our commercial bank represent part of the liquid *assets* of the public. It is equally true that the cash *assets* of our commercial bank represent the *liabilities* of the central bank.[2] Such liabilities may take two forms: banknotes issued by the central bank or a credit balance in the books of the central bank. Commercial banks hold part of their total cash reserve in each of these forms. Holdings of notes constitute their till money, ready at hand to meet the demands of customers who wish to draw out cash (that is, to convert their deposits into notes). In the same way, the commercial banks can obtain notes to replenish their till money by drawing on their balances at the central bank.

Hence the central bank stands in almost exactly the same relation to the commercial banks as that in which the banks stand in relation to the public. Just as a balance with a commercial bank is of value to its customers ultimately for the reason that the balance can be converted into legal tender money on demand, so a balance at the central bank is of value to a commercial bank for precisely the same reason. If the central bank is to be certain of meeting any demands for cash made

1. See Chapters VIII and IX.

2. It will be remembered we assumed that, prior to the formation of the bank, notes represented the only form of money, i.e., coin is ignored for the present purpose.

upon it by its banker-customers, it must itself hold a reserve of notes; but in order to meet that obligation to provide cash on demand the central bank does not need, any more than the commercial banks, to keep the whole of its assets in the form of notes. In other words, the central bank, too, can safely 'pyramid' on the basis of its note holding – that is, up to a certain point it can without undue risk acquire assets other than cash ('securities'), and so incur liabilities in excess of its cash reserve. Like the commercial banks, again, the central bank must in principle pay regard to the proportion between its cash reserve and its deposit liabilities. Indeed, before the war this Proportion was normally higher than the cash ratio of the commercial banks, though subject to fluctuations.

One point in the above may seem a little puzzling. We first spoke of the notes as 'issued by' the central bank, and then said that the central bank must hold a reserve of notes. Does it have any meaning to speak as though the bank of issue and the central bank were quite separate institutions, although we have implied that they are one and the same? The answer is that there is no inherent reason why the note-issuing authority should also be the central bank; there can be, for example, such things as Treasury notes. Though normally combined, issuing notes and conducting a central bank are in principle quite distinct functions. And it so happens that the two functions are kept quite distinct in the British monetary system. Although both functions are performed by the Bank of England, the Bank itself has a split personality. For historical reasons it is divided into two Departments – the Issue Department and the Banking Department – which from some points of view might just as well be separate institutions. It is vital always to bear in mind this statutory schizophrenia of the Bank of England, and in speaking of the Bank to be quite clear whether one is referring to the Issue Department or the Banking Department. It is, in fact, the latter which holds the reserve balances of the commercial banks, and which needs to hold a reserve of the notes issued by the Issue Department in order to be sure of meeting its obligations to these banks and its other customers.

Naturally, the ordinary rules of book-keeping apply to the Issue Department just as much as to any other institution. If the Issue Department issues notes and so incurs liabilities,[1] then it must necessarily acquire exactly equivalent assets so that its accounts balance. Indeed, the issuing of notes may be regarded as a process of buying assets and paying for them with pieces of paper which the community finds it convenient to use as money. The nature of the assets acquired will depend on the country's exchange régime. Under a gold standard in its purest form the notes might be matched pound for pound by gold, i.e., gold would then be the only asset the Issue Department would be prepared to acquire. Even in gold standard days, however, a certain number of notes were issued in exchange not for gold but for Government obligations – the so-called fiduciary issue. Since 1931, holders of Bank of England notes have not been entitled to demand gold in exchange for them, but until September 1939 a substantial proportion of the country's gold reserve continued to be held in the Issue Department. On the outbreak of war the entire gold holding was transferred to the Exchange Equalization Account, with the exception of a small driblet which still figures in the Bank return as a reminder of happier days. Since 1939, therefore, the fiduciary issue has represented virtually the entire note issue.

Fortunately, the value of a currency has no *direct* connection whatever with its 'backing'. If the issue of a pure paper currency were limited in precisely the same way as one based upon gold, then there is no reason why the value of the paper currency should not be identical with that of the currency with 100 per cent gold 'backing' – so long as the public could be brought to realize that fact, or at all events to place confidence in the management of the currency. One element in maintaining confidence is to ensure that additions to the note issue are not made too light-heartedly. Before 1914 there were no provisions for increasing the fiduciary issue as a normal procedure[2] but, inevitably, the war of 1914–18 brought a sweeping increase. The question of the expanded note issue received much attention in the years which followed. In 1928 provision was made

1. We shall examine later what that phrase means in this context. See Chapter XI.

2. Small increases took place from time to time under the mechanism of the 1844 Act, but only in partial replacement of lapsed issues of private banks.

for flexibility in the fiduciary issue, but through an elaborate procedure to ensure that Parliament would have the opportunity of discussing any increases.[1]

We have now had a brief glimpse of the three main elements in our banking structure: the Issue Department of the Bank of England, the Banking Department and the commercial banks. One final point remains to be noted and then we can proceed to construct a crude working model of the system in operation. It is that in the normal course the commercial banks and the Banking Department are the channels through which the notes issued by the Issue Department reach the public. To take a typical example, a business firm may draw notes from its bank to pay the wages of its workpeople, and the bank may replenish its till money by drawing on its balance at the Bank of England. Hence a homely parallel may serve to impress on the reader the basic functions, in relation to the supply of cash, of the three elements in the system. We can think of the Issue Department as the *manufacturer* of the notes, of the Banking Department as the *wholesaler* distributing the notes to the commercial banks, and of the commercial banks as *retailers* keeping a stock of notes for the convenience of their customers.

II

Now to erect our simplified working model of the pyramid of credit, omitting any details which do not affect the basic principles and making a number of unrealistic assumptions purely for purposes of convenience. We will suppose that our *Issue Department* has created £500 millions of notes against assets whose nature, as we have seen, is of little importance in a developed community.[2] Of the total note issue, £400 millions are described in the Bank return as 'notes in circulation'; in fact, £150 millions constitute the till money of the commercial banks and £250 millions are in the hands of the public. The remaining £100 millions of notes (not 'in circula-

1. See page 29.

2. One should not, of course, confuse the possession of a gold reserve (and its use for comparatively rational purposes such as the settlement of international transactions) with the use of gold as a 'backing' for notes.

tion') are held by the *Banking Department* as its sole reserve. Let us assume that the Banking Department works to a Proportion (i.e., ratio of reserve to deposit liabilities), of 33 per cent. That is, it will hold £200 millions of other assets ('securities') whose nature need not concern us at this point, and will therefore have deposit liabilities totalling £300 millions. Of these we will suppose £150 millions to represent the balances at the

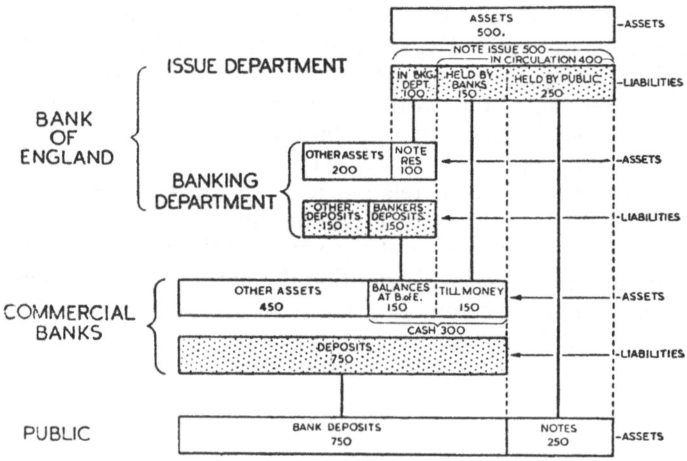

Diagram 1

Bank of England of the *commercial banks*. Since we have already endowed the banks with £150 millions of notes as till money, this means that their total cash reserve is £300 millions. If, to suit our convenience, they maintain the remarkably high cash ratio of 40 per cent, they will hold £450 millions of other assets and have deposit liabilities of £750 millions. Together with its £250 millions of notes, these £750 millions of bank deposits constitute the monetary assets of the *public*. At this point the double-entry book-keeping comes to an end for, in this context at any rate, the public have no liabilities.

The particulars given are sufficient to enable us to build up a complete outline picture of the monetary situation in our hypothetical economy. The skeleton balance sheets of the three 'strata' in the banking system are as follows:

ISSUE DEPARTMENT

Liabilities	£m	*Assets*	£m
Notes:			
In circulation ..	400	Securities	500
In Banking Dept. ..	100		
Total	500		500

BANKING DEPARTMENT

Liabilities	£m	*Assets*	£m
Bankers' deposits ..	150	Reserve (notes) ..	100
'Other' deposits ..	150	Securities	200
Total	300	Total	300

COMMERCIAL BANKS

Liabilities	£m	*Assets*	£m
Deposits	750	Cash in hand (£150 millions) and at Bank of England (£150 millions)	300
		Securities	450
Total	750	Total	750

One very significant thing about this picture (set out in Diagram 1), is the way we skip from one side of the balance sheet to the other as we move down from one stratum to the next: part of the note *liabilities* of the Issue Department constitute the cash *assets* (the Reserve) of the Banking Department; part of the deposit *liabilities* of the Banking Department supplement till money to make up the cash *assets* (reserves) of the commercial banks; and the deposit *liabilities* of the commercial banks represent the chief monetary *assets* of the public. This alternation of assets and liabilities is brought out very clearly in Diagram 1 on p. 20, which also illustrates more clearly than can any amount of description the functional relationship between the various elements in the system. It is a diagram that should be studied with care, since a firm grasp of the principles it embodies is essential to any real understanding of currency and credit.

The reader will observe, for example, that while the total note issue is only £500 millions, the total money holdings of the public are exactly double that amount, or £1,000 millions. Only one-quarter of this total consists of notes directly held by the public. The bank deposits which make up the remainder of the money stock are, even on our very unreal assumptions, three times as great as the remaining £250 millions of notes held by the banking system – the Reserve of the Banking Department and the till money of the commercial banks – and which provide the basis of this pyramid of credit.

What are the factors which govern the relationship between the note issue and the stock of money in the hands of the public? There are some additional influences that need not trouble us at this stage, but the diagram shows the factors which are normally decisive. The successive links in the chain are:

(1) The proportion of the note issue held by the public, the commercial banks and the Banking Department, respectively.
(2) The Proportion maintained by the Banking Department which, given the size of its Reserve, determines the size of its total deposit liabilities.
(3) The proportion of the Banking Department's total deposit liabilities which represents the balances of the commericial banks.
(4) The cash ratio of the commercial banks.

It is at once apparent that the 'cash ratio' of the Banking Department – the Proportion – and the cash ratios of the commercial banks are of special importance. If instead of assuming a 40 per cent cash ratio for the commercial banks we had employed the actual cash ratio of 8 per cent at which they now aim, the volume of bank deposits would be increased from £750 millions to £3,750 millions, and the total money stock to £4,000 millions, or eight times the assumed note issue.[1] That part of

1. In 1963, the amount of coin and Bank of England notes outstanding averaged £2,440 millions, of which it is estimated that £2,220 millions were held by the public. The Reserve of the Banking Department averaged £43 millions and the till money held by the clearing banks £399 millions. Total clearing bank cash (including their balances with the Bank of England) averaged £647 millions, to give a ratio to deposits of 8.1 per cent. The deposit liabilities of the Banking Department averaged £334 millions to give a Proportion of 13·0 per cent.

the note issue held by the banking system at any moment has there-fore an immeasurably greater significance than notes in the hands of the public. When they are actually passing from hand to hand, notes are little more than small change, used only for wage payments, retail purchases and other small transactions, and therefore of not enormously greater monetary importance than the token coinage. Under classical conditions, on the other hand, notes in the hands of the banking system govern the volume of bank deposits,[1] which make up by far the greater part of the total money stock in a developed community and, when transferred from one depositor to another, constitute the means of payment for by far the larger part of the community's transactions.

This dual rôle performed by the note issue is of fundamental importance. Let us suppose that the banks work to a cash ratio of 10 per cent and that £10 millions of notes are withdrawn. If that cash cannot be replaced, deposits will have to fall by £100 millions, i.e., the banks' 'other assets' must be reduced by £90 millions to restore the cash ratio.

We can gain useful insight into the workings of the system by looking at the repercussions of a mere change in the preferences of the public as to how much of a given money stock it wishes to hold in the form of notes. Starting from the position set out in the diagram, let us see what happens if the public decides to hold £300 millions of notes instead of £250 millions

Various possible effects of this decision are summarized in Table I on page 24. The figures in the first column correspond, on both the liabilities and the assets side, with those in the diagram. Stage II shows what happens if the banks supply the extra £50 millions of notes out of their till money. The banks' customers obtain the extra notes by drawing on their balances with the banks, and in providing the notes the banks extinguish £50 millions of their former liabilities to their customers; bank deposits are thus reduced to £700 millions. But the banks' till

1. Complications are introduced if other assets held by the banks, such as Treasury bills, are automatically convertible into cash. See Chapters IV, VIII and XI, where it is shown that in our system cash normally can be replaced in fact by calling in loans from the money market or allowing Treasury bills to run off. The effect is that the liquidity ratio (see p. 78) is now of greater ultimate significance than the ratio of cash to deposits.

TABLE I.—EFFECT OF NOTE WITHDRAWALS

LIABILITIES	Stage I	Stage II	Stage III	Stage IV	ASSETS	Stage I	Stage II	Stage III	Stage IV
Issue Department:									
Notes in circulation	400	No change	450	450	Securities	500	No change	No change	550
Notes in banking Department	100	No change	50	100					
	500	—	500	550					
Banking Department:									
Bankers' deposits ..	150	No change	100	No change	Reserve	100	No change	50	100
'Other' deposits	150	No change	150	No change	Securities	200	No change	200	150
	300		250			300		250	250
Commercial Banks:									
Deposits	750	700	700	No change	Till money	150	100	150	No change
					Balances at B/E ..	150	150	100	No change
					Total cash	300	250	250	
					Securities	450	450	450	No change
						750	700	700	
Public:									
					Notes	250	300	300	No change
					Bank deposits ..	750	700	700	No change
					Total liquid assets ..	1,000	1,000	1,000	

money has fallen to £100 millions and their total cash to £250 millions, which means that the ratio of cash to deposits has fallen from 40 per cent to something under 36 per cent. If the banks wished to restore the former ratio of 40 per cent, therefore, they would have to reduce their *other* assets by £75 millions, causing a further decline in deposits to only £625 millions.

Up to this point, neither the Banking Department nor the Issue Department has come into the picture. Suppose, however, that instead of allowing their till money to fall the commercial banks replenish their tills – as they normally would – with £50 millions of notes obtained by drawing on their balances at the Bank of England (Stage III). This reduces the Reserve from £100 millions to £50 millions, bankers' deposits from £150 millions to £100 millions, and the total deposit liabilities of the Banking Department from £300 millions to £250 millions. In other words, the Proportion has fallen from 33 per cent to 20 per cent. To restore the Proportion the Banking Department would have to unload £100 millions of other assets. Assuming these are bought either by the banks or the public (not by the Banking Department's other customers, the owners of 'other' deposits), the commercial banks' cash holdings will fall to £150 millions. To maintain a 40 per cent cash ratio, bank deposits must therefore be reduced to no more than £375 millions.

So we see that a mere decision of the public to hold 5 per cent more of its total money holdings in the form of notes and 5 per cent less in the form of bank deposits could necessitate the extinction of half of the total bank deposits in existence, even with the very modest amount of pyramiding implied by our absurdly high bank cash ratio of 40 per cent, if the commercial banks maintained a constant cash ratio and were unable to restore their cash holdings by obtaining central bank credit in exchange for other assets. It is true, on the other hand, that our assumed withdrawals of £50 millions of notes represent the inconceivably large increase of 20 per cent overnight in the demand for currency. But appreciable variations in the demand for currency do occur over fairly short periods for well-understood reasons that have nothing to do with the general level of the national income: for example, the quite substantial seasonal withdrawals during the summer holiday period and to finance

Christmas spending. Hence a banking system in which the central bank held its Proportion absolutely rigid would obviously be subject to the most frightful jolts and jars. Indeed, it is precisely one of the primary duties of the central bank to cushion these shocks to the credit structure by allowing its ratio to vary. On the other hand, the central banks' control of the monetary situation was traditionally dependent on the commercial banks keeping their cash ratio fixed within very narrow limits.

What complicates matters is that a withdrawal of notes may take place for three different sorts of reasons which have fundamentally different implications for banking policy:

(a) The notes may be wanted, as we have seen, to finance spending of a kind that cannot conveniently be settled by cheque, and which is higher at some periods than others:
(b) the public may not want to use the notes for spending at all, but may simply want to hold a larger quantity of idle currency than usual (e.g., fear that communications may be interrupted by air raids or, in former times, fear for the solvency of the banks, leading to a 'run' on them), or
(c) the volume of transactions to be settled by notes may have risen because of an expansion in the national income.

In the first two cases the only duty of the central bank is obviously to make available the extra notes which the public wants, for no questions of monetary policy are involved. In the third case, on the other hand, the central bank might in some circumstances justifiably regard the increase in money incomes as inflationary, and seek to damp it down by reducing the volume of bank deposits. To decide whether it should take such action, or on the contrary remain entirely passive in the face of any particular withdrawal and permit an appropriate fall in its Proportion, thus presents the central bank with a nice problem of interpretation. Inevitably, it has not always hit on the right answer.

To return to Table I, the only effect on the Issue Department of the original Stage III transaction is that the transfer of £50 millions of notes from the Banking Department to the commercial banks will be reflected (unlike a transfer of notes from the banks to the public), as an increase – from £400 millions to £450 millions – in notes described as 'in circulation'. In Stage IV we suppose that the Banking Department replenishes its Reserve by obtaining notes from the Issue Department. This it does by handing £50 millions of 'other assets' to the Issue Department in exchange for additional notes which have to be created. This transaction, unlike all the others we have examined, thus involves an increase in the total note *issue* to £550 millions. The counterpart of the new notes on the other side of the Issue Department's balance sheet is, of course, the £50 millions of assets handed over by the Banking Department in exchange for the notes. It will be noted that the effect of this operation has been to raise the Proportion from 20 per cent to 40 per cent. If the Banking Department were content merely to restore its original Proportion of 33 per cent, an increase of £25 millions in the note issue would suffice.

We have thus seen two alternative ways in which the Banking Department can, if it wishes, maintain its Proportion in the face of an increased demand for notes on the part of the public: First, it can sell 'other assets', which may necessitate a contraction of a far larger amount in bank deposits if the commercial banks have no surplus of liquid assets.[1] Or secondly, the necessity for such sales, with their resultant contraction in bank deposits, will be avoided if the Banking Department can obtain new notes from the Issue Department through an increase in the total note issue. Whether for better or worse, it clearly matters a great deal which of these alternatives is adopted, for except in a completely controlled economy the size of the money stock will strongly influence, if it does not determine, the levels of production and the national income. Naturally, therefore, the conditions on which notes can be created or extinguished have been carefully regulated by law. Unfortunately, no similar control is imposed on the issue of Treasury bills, which nowa-

1. It is shown later (see p. 43) that this contraction in the assets of the Banking Department can be implemented, if at all, only with the assistance of a rise in Bank Rate.

days comprise (directly or indirectly) the greater part of the liquid assets of the banks and represent claims to cash at one remove (see Chapter VIII).

Under the gold standard in its purest form, as has been seen, the only asset that the Issue Department would normally be empowered to accept would be gold, though in thinking of the gold standard we usually lay even greater stress on the obverse fact: that the Issue Department was bound to pay out gold freely in order to redeem its notes when called upon to do so. This inter-convertibility of notes and gold, of course, meant that the size of the note issue, and at one remove the volume of bank credit, was directly geared to the country's external balance of payments; for a favourable balance of payments would bring an influx of gold and increase the Banking Department's Reserve, while an adverse balance would call for an export of gold obtained by presenting notes for payment in gold.

That did not make the gold standard the wonderful self-equilibrating mechanism that so many people still believe it to have been. Nevertheless, if a country's whole policy is directed towards maintaining a particular rate of exchange, it is *a priori* reasonable that the money supply should be expanded when the external position is strong, and conversely. Provided the influx or efflux of gold reflects a surplus or deficit in the current balance of payments, indeed, such a response is wholly appropriate. Even if the gold influx represents the counterpart of an inflow of capital seeking genuine investment, it will cause no great problems: for such capital is unlikely to be withdrawn again within a very short period, and its investment in physical assets will be facilitated by an expansion in the stock of money and therefore, at a further remove, in the level of incomes.

The case is obviously different where the incoming gold reflects merely an influx of short-term funds seeking a temporary haven, such as the 'funk money' whose flights from one international centre to another caused so much havoc in the inter-war period.[1] If it were thought likely that the funds would be withdrawn and the gold be lost again at short notice, the central bank in the receiving country would not allow the incoming gold to form a net addition to its assets, thus initiating a

1. And which precipitated the 1961 crisis (see Chapter XVII).

multiple expansion of commercial bank credit. It would offset the gold influx in whole or in part by sales of securities, allowing its Proportion to rise. If the gold influx were completely neutralized by sales of securities the total assets of the central bank would be unchanged and the domestic credit situation also be unaffected. In this procedure we see the informal beginnings of a technique of neutralization which reached its ultimate refinement with the institution of Exchange Equalization Accounts by this and other countries (see Chapter X).

Recent history, in short, casts doubt on the tacit assumption of the 1844 Bank Charter Act that it is in all circumstances perfectly safe and desirable to expand the note issue, provided the additional notes are backed twenty shillings in the pound by gold. On the other hand, it is obviously a momentous step, under any exchange régime, to divorce changes in the note issue from movements in the country's gold reserve, since gold is still the only universally acceptable means of payment, and hence the only sure means of settling an adverse balance of payments with the rest of the world. It is only to be expected, therefore, that Parliament should exercise a special supervision over the creation of notes against assets other than gold, i.e., over increases in the fiduciary issue, though little or nothing may in fact be achieved by this unless the issue of floating debt is also carefully controlled (see pages 44–5, 120–3).

The Currency and Bank Notes Act of 1928 laid down a basic level for the fiduciary issue of £260 millions but with provision for flexibility. On the representations of the Bank of England, the Treasury was empowered to sanction a change in the fiduciary issue for a period of not more than six months by a Minute to be laid before both Houses of Parliament. The Treasury sanction could be renewed but if the issue remained above the basic figure for a period of two years or more the approval of Parliament was required. This procedure was not affected by the Currency and Bank Notes Act of early 1939, which in other respects radically modified the principle on which the issue had been regulated since 1844.[1]

1. See Chapter XI.

CHAPTER III

THE BASIS OF CREDIT

In the previous chapter it was shown that a banking system in which the central bank sought to maintain a constant Proportion would be subject to very severe jolts and jars. Let us now look rather more closely at the sources of these shocks, and what the central bank must do to neutralize them or cushion their impact. That is, we are to discuss the mechanics of day-to-day 'credit policy', as it is called, and not monetary policy, which is something else again. It is true that precisely similar operations by the central bank may subserve either credit policy or monetary policy, or for that matter both at the same time: but the objects of credit policy and of monetary policy are very different.

One might say that in credit policy we take the level of national income for granted. We are concerned only to *prevent* fortuitous and unwanted fluctuations in the flow of spending as the result of temporary or fortuitous changes in the supply of or demand for cash, changes which, if the central bank maintained a rigid Proportion, could lead to still sharper fluctuations in the total stock of money. With monetary policy, the approach is reversed. We are then considering how to *induce* desired changes in the level of national income by varying the supply of cash and thereby inducing changes in the total stock of money, with the object, in turn, of influencing in the desired direction the level of spending.

Monetary policy, in other words, is designed to secure positive results over a longish period, credit policy to prevent meaningless and disturbing fluctuations in the short period. The two are inter-dependent. If the object of monetary policy is to keep the level of national income exactly stable, for example, this does not mean that the central bank can remain merely passive.

On the contrary, this stability over a period could not be secured unless the Bank were following an active and vigilant credit policy. Indeed, the central bank might have to follow at times a strongly expansionist credit policy to prevent a violent contraction in incomes as the result of seasonal or other increases in the demand for currency. Monetary policy, in short, is concerned with trends, credit policy with preventing or smoothing out short-period deviations from the desired trend.

These are mere generalizations which cannot convey a great deal until we have seen what they mean in concrete terms. For that, we must focus our attention on the section of the Bank return which shows the assets and liabilities of the Banking Department. Any recent return will serve for purposes of illustration, and we reproduce that showing the position as at the close of business on Thursday, February 8th, 1962:

BANKING DEPARTMENT

	£		£
Capital	14,553,000	Government securities	455,594,624
Rest	3,804,070	Other securities:	
Public deposits (including Exchequer, Savings Banks, Commissioners of National Debt, and Dividend Accounts)	10,907,864	Discount and Advances £78,112,868	
		Securities £19,004,977	97,117,845
Special Deposits ..	241,400,000	Notes	26,798,134
Other deposits:		Coin	864,718
Bankers £241,593,101			
Other Accounts £68,117,286	309,710,387		
	£580,375,321		£580,375,321

Dated this 8th day of February, 1962 L. K. O'Brien, *Chief Cashier.*

It will be seen that the liabilities side comprises five items. We are not concerned at present with the item Capital, which is constant, or the Rest (undistributed profits), which fluctuates little, neither having any great monetary significance. The remaining four items make up the Bank's total deposit liabilities.

The relatively new item 'Special Deposits' (first seen in the

Return for May 11th, 1960) represent funds which the clearing and Scottish banks have been required, for reasons of monetary policy, to lodge with the central bank and which cease to count among their liquid assets.[1]

The remaining items, taken together, make up the normal credit base. 'Other accounts' – usually fairly stable – comprise the balances of overseas governments, sterling area central banks and of the Bank's few remaining private customers. Public deposits (the working balances of public departments in the widest sense) are in practice kept at a low level but in principle are liable to sharp fluctuations arising out of movements of funds between the public and the government. Every payment from the private to the public sector is potentially a transfer of funds from bankers' deposits into public deposits, and conversely. Payments in one direction largely offset payments in the other, however, and it is only the *net* movement of funds which affects the credit situation.

Let us suppose that on a particular day the only such transaction is the payment of £1 million of taxes by a company keeping an account with one of the clearing banks. The company draws its cheque for £1 million in favour of the Inland Revenue; when the cheque is presented the clearing bank pays it by giving the Inland Revenue its own draft on the Bank of England for £1 million, debiting its customer. Hence the final position is that the clearing bank's cash reserve and deposit liabilities are each reduced by £1 million, while within the Banking Department there will be a fall of £1 million in bankers' deposits and a rise of £1 million in public deposits. In practice, an individual transaction of this kind is likely to be swamped in a multitude of others, and the channels of settlement will be less direct. But the principle is clear: other things equal, an excess of payments by the public to the departments will deplete bank cash, and conversely.

The fact that the Government keeps its main accounts with the central bank, and not with any of the commercial banks thus has important monetary consequences, making necessary a technique of credit management much more elaborate than would otherwise be the case. Let us suppose that the Govern-

1. See Appendix.

ment were to keep accounts with the commercial banks (as is done, for example, in the United States), and were to allow balances to pile up to its credit. Neither the cash reserves nor the deposits of the commercial banks would show any change, but a larger share of the outstanding deposits would have moved into the ownership of the Government, leaving less for the public. This depletion of the liquid assets of the public would be deflationary in tendency, but not to an extent comparable with the violently deflationary effect of a similar accumulation of liquid funds by the departments under our system. Constant vigilance is thus needed to ensure that if the Government is tending to accumulate cash on public deposits the funds are promptly returned to the commercial banks (or, more rarely, replaced by an addition to the total deposit liabilities of the Banking Department).

That is one of the main *objects* of credit policy, and it is simple enough, but an explanation of the *techniques* of credit policy must be deferred until we have gained some conception of the discount market and its functions. One point may, however, be mentioned here. It will be noted that nothing was said of any converse problem arising out of a running down of public deposits with a consequent increase in bank cash reserves. This was because there does not in fact exist complete symmetry in this respect, since the aim is to keep public deposits down to something like a minimum working balance. If the Government has suddenly to make payments in excess of its current receipts from the public, therefore, it will not normally be able to effect these by running down a cash balance already in hand; it will have to borrow the money.

Like anybody else requiring temporary accommodation, it will probably raise the funds in the first instance from its banker, in this case the Bank of England. This will be reflected in a rise in public deposits, having its counterpart on the assets side of the Bank return in an addition to 'Government securities'. As soon as the funds are raised, however, they will be paid out to the public, and the additional credit will find its way into bankers' deposits, by a chain of transactions reversing those described above. A continuance of this process would clearly be as inflationary in tendency as a locking up of funds on public deposits is deflationary. It may be that the Government's need for funds is a purely temporary one, and that the advance can be paid off out of a revenue surplus after a short interval and the additional credit extinguished. If, however, the Government's deficit is a more persistent one – as in war-time, for example – it will need to borrow, either from the commercial banks or direct from the public, in order to repay at least part of its initial borrowings from the Bank of England. This process and its implications will be analysed later. They touch on very wide questions indeed: namely, the whole problems of deficit finance and of the control of interest rates.

Let us now turn to the assets side of the return. Of the five items, the last two – notes and coin – comprise the Reserve. The remaining three represent Securities, divided into Government Securities (i.e., obligations of the British Government), and Other Securities, which in turn are subdivided under two headings, namely, 'Discounts and Advances' and 'Other Securities, Securities.' Although the latter items are bracketed in the Return, there is an important distinction between them. It is that 'Other Securities, Securities' represent assets acquired on the initiative of the Bank itself. Discounts and advances, on the other hand, represent assets acquired when the Bank is asked for a loan by any of its private customers; and in practice such a request from one special group of customers – the discount market – cannot be refused. A rise in this item – at the end of June or December, for instance – is likely to indicate stringent conditions in the money market; for advances by the Bank of England to the discount market, as we shall see in greater detail later, are the traditional means by which such a stringency is relieved. It is the very essence of central banking that the Bank should at all times be willing to act as lender of last resort against suitable securities – a principle only established, nevertheless, at the cost of a series of painful crises during the last century.

Movements in Government securities, too, may represent the acquisition of assets other than on the Bank's own initiative, namely, Ways and Means advances to the Exchequer; for, in addition to the discount market, the Bank has this other customer, the Government, whose requests for accommodation cannot in practice be refused.[1] For the Bank to do so would have been almost unthinkable long before the transfer of the Bank to public ownership on March 1st, 1946. Nevertheless, the Bank's control of the monetary situation could obviously be undermined by excessive short-term Government borrowing. And since nobody would surely deny, even in these days, that the Bank bears *some* responsibility, even if not the ultimate responsibility, for the soundness of our money, it seems obviously reasonable that any representations of the Governor should carry great weight with any responsible Government. In its fundamentals, that situation was clearly not changed in any way by the change of ownership. Even now, therefore, it would most certainly be incorrect to regard the Governor as the Chancellor's factotum and the Bank merely as the Threadneedle Street branch of the Treasury. Constitutionally, it is true, the Governor can do no more than advise; but then, in strict theory, Ministers themselves merely advise the Crown. In the last analysis, the whole question of the balance of power between Whitehall and Threadneedle Street comes down to one simple issue: Whose resignation would be the more embarrassing to the government of the day – that of the Chancellor or of the Governor?

However, we are verging on issues that carry us far beyond the mechanics of credit policy, which are our present preoccupation. The objective, it will be recalled, is to prevent disturbing short-period fluctuations in bank cash and hence at one remove in the volume of bank deposits. Since till money is normally maintained at a very stable minimum working level, the variable element in bank cash reserves is their balances with the Bank of England. Arithmetically, therefore, the aim of credit policy can be expressed quite simply. We have seen that significant fluctuations in the Banking Department's liabilities are normally confined to public deposits and bankers'

1. In some systems limitations are placed on direct lending by the central bank to the Government, e.g., in the United States direct loans by the Federal Reserve Banks were authorized in 1942 as a war-time measure up to a specific limit of $5 billions (see National City Bank monthly letter, September 1950). But central banks almost invariably buy and sell government securities in the open market; any such purchases indirectly support government credit in the same way as direct loans, and can have the same inflationary implications.

deposits. It follows that changes in the Banking Department's total assets (that is, in the Reserve plus Securities), are usually associated with equal changes in public deposits plus bankers' deposits.

If public deposits could be depended upon to remain stable, the problem would be simpler still. Any change in the total assets of the Banking Department would then be associated with an equal change in bankers' deposits, while the lattter would be completely stabilized if the total assets of the Banking Department were completely stabilized: that is, if any reduction in the Reserve were offset by equivalent acquisitions of securities, and conversely. This part of credit policy is, in fact, put into operation almost automatically to neutralize seasonal fluctuations in the demand for currency, as may be illustrated by the following example:

Date	Notes in Circulation £m	*Banking Department*			
		Assets		*Liabilities*	
		Reserve £m	Securities £m	Total Deposits £m	Bankers' Deposits £m
1947					
Mar. 12	1,385·4	65.6	346·5	393·7	289·4
Aug. 6	1,421·7	31·0	381·1	393·7	279·6
Changes:	+36·3	−34·6	+34·6	Nil	−9·8

Let us now consider a slightly more complicated example:

Date	Notes in Circulation £m	*Banking Department*			
		Assets		*Liabilities*	
		Reserve £m	Securities £m	Total Deposits £m	Bankers' Deposits £m
1959					
Sept. 23	2,102·9	23·3	325·8	330·6	252·9
Dec. 30	2,237·0	64·2	287·5	333·5	255·3
Changes:	+134·1	+40·9	−38·3	+2·9	+2·4

Over this period, it will be seen, the note circulation rose by as much as £134 millions, yet over the same period the Reserve *increased* by £41 millions. The explanation is, of course, that in the meantime there had been increases totalling £175 millions in the fiduciary issue (from £2,125 millions to £2,300 millions). On balance, however, the reduction in the securities holding was a little less than the increase in the Reserve, so that the basis of credit was little changed by these large movements in the note circulation and in the fiduciary issue. How these operations affect the Bank Return will be seen more clearly if between the actual figures shown in the returns for October 28th and November 4th, for example, we insert those that would have been seen if the *only* movement during the week had been the fiduciary issue increase:

	Bank return Oct. 28, 1959 £m	After increase in fiduciary issue £m	Change £m	Actual changes shown by Nov. 4 return £m	Hence, effect of other changes during week £m
Reserve ..	19·2	69·2	+50·0	+37·3	−12·7
Securities ..	344·1	294·1	−50·0	−36·7	+13·3
Deposits ..	345·6	345·6	Nil	+ ·6	+ ·6

In the opening days of 1960 the note circulation declined sufficiently to permit the restoration of the fiduciary issue to £2,200 millions. The Bank return changes associated with this operation were as follows:

	Bank return Dec. 30 1959 £m	Bank return Jan. 6 1960 £m	Change £m	Effect of reduction in fiduciary issue £m	Hence, effect of other changes during week £m
Reserve ..	64·2	15·9	−48·3	−100.0	+51·7
Securities ..	287·5	326·2	+38·7	+100.0	−61·3
Deposits ..	333·5	323·9	−10·4	Nil	−10·4

It may be noted that in this week bankers' deposits fell by about the same amount as total deposits, a small increase in public deposits being offset by a small decline in 'other accounts'. It is, of course, only if the combined total of these two other items remains stable that a policy of stabilizing the total deposit liabilities of the Banking Department will also serve to stabilize bankers' deposits, and therefore the basis of commercial bank credit.

While normally maintained at a low figure representing the minimum convenient working balance for the Departments, public deposits do rise sharply from time to time. If that happens, bankers' deposits will be correspondingly reduced unless the *total* deposits of the Banking Department are increased by an expansion of its total assets. Before the war, however, the Bank seemed most reluctant to expand its assets in order to offset temporary contractions in bank cash due to the immobilization of funds on public deposits. An example is to be seen in the changes between September and October 1936, as set out in the following table:

	Average Sept. 2–Sept. 23, 1936 £m	Average Sept. 30–Oct. 28, 1936 £m	Change £m
Public deposits ..	15·9	34·3	+18·4
Bankers' deposits ..	102·8	79·1	−23·7
Other accounts ..	38·5	41·1	+ 2·6
Total deposits ..	157·2	154·5	− 2·7

The sharp rise in public deposits, and the resulting depletion of bankers' deposits, were due to a sudden efflux of funds from this country following the gold bloc devaluations of 1936. The Exchange Equalization Account was receiving large sums in payment for sales of gold, and the technical arrangements for returning these funds promptly to the banks had not yet been perfected. Though the Bank was sharply criticized at the time, it is clear in retrospect that the stringency caused relatively little disturbance to the banking situation, for bank deposits actually rose during the month. Nevertheless, this meant that in their October return the clearing banks were forced to show, for the first time since the 1914–18 war, a published ratio below 10 per cent, while the tender Treasury bill rate – the most sensitive index, as we shall see later, of pressure on bank cash reserves – rose slightly. Since 1939, however, a technique of credit control so flexible and refined has been elaborated for the very purpose of dealing with large displacements of funds between the banking system and Government departments that the problem of immobilizations has quite receded into the background.

To sum up, we can say that before the war the Bank was usually most expeditious in neutralizing currency movements by stabilizing its total assets, but equally slow to expand its total assets if bankers' deposits should be depleted by the immobilization of funds on public deposits.

CHAPTER IV

SOME FUNDAMENTALS OF CENTRAL BANKING

IN the last chapter we saw that the central bank seeks to influence the volume of bank credit (and hence at one remove – except in a completely controlled economy – the level of the national income) by regulating bankers' deposits; and that the level of bankers' deposits, in turn, is closely related to the level of the total assets of the Banking Department. Every withdrawal of currency into circulation reduces both the Reserve and bankers' deposits, and conversely. Given the stability of commercial bank cash ratios which is a basic feature of the system, therefore, currency movements would have a most disturbing tendency if the Bank were not able to counteract them by compensating changes in the other assets of the Banking Department, i.e., by purchases and sales of securities. But the real problems are, of course, connected not with seasonal and other temporary movements but with secular trends. The level of the Reserve, as we have seen, is geared to the demand for currency on the part of the public, and a sustained increase in that demand could eliminate the Reserve completely.

What happens then? In practice, the Banking Department can always obtain additional notes by selling securities to the Issue Department. That was true even in the gold standard days of the nineteenth century, though in those days a 'suspension of the Bank Act' to permit an emergency increase in the fiduciary issue was a rare and a momentous step. The Issue Department was precluded under the Bank Charter Act of 1844 from issuing any notes in excess of the fixed fiduciary issue except in exchange for gold. Under that régime the Reserve of the Banking Department, even if it was held in the form of notes, represented the Bank's only free gold reserve. It was the counterpart of that portion of the total gold reserve (held in the Issue Department) which was not locked up as backing for notes *in circulation*, and therefore the only gold immediately available for the settlement of international transactions. While the country was on the gold standard, in fact, the Reserve was vulnerable not only to an increase in the demand for currency on the part of the domestic population (an internal drain) but also to an adverse balance of international payments (an external drain). By a well-known mechanism,[1] an adverse balance would cause notes to be presented in exchange for gold which would then be exported. While this process continued the Bank return would show, as regards the Issue Department, a parallel decline in the gold holding and the total note issue and, as regards the Banking Department, a parallel decline in the Reserve and in bankers' deposits.

Should the reserve stand in danger of exhaustion, the situation could be saved, in the last extremity, by the suspension of the Bank Act, i.e., by temporary permission to the Bank to increase the fiduciary issue beyond the fixed limit. This procedure in effect released gold hitherto immobilized as backing for notes in circulation and enabled the Banking Department to replenish its Reserve by transferring securities to the Issue Department.

If the drain were an internal one, due, for example, to one of the recurring panics which punctuated the century, the demand would probably not be for gold as such but for notes to hold as liquid reserves, to effect repayment in legal tender of debts falling due, or to meet the demands of nervous bank depositors who preferred for the time being to hold cash. To meet such a run, the commercial banks would require to convert into notes their balances with the Banking Department (whose total liabilities would greatly exceed the depleted Reserve). Indeed, they would probably find these balances insuffi-

1. The Bank was under obligation to buy gold at £3 17s. 9d. per standard ounce and sell it at £3 17s. 10½d. If the balance of payments was adverse, the external value of sterling would decline to a point at which it became profitable, notwithstanding shipping and interest costs, to present notes to the Bank for payment in gold and export the gold for resale at the (higher) price now obtainable in foreign currency.

cient at such a time, and the Bank would be pressed to create additional cash by lending freely (not direct to the commercial banks but to the discount market or other traders[1]), thus adding to its liabilities and to the potential demands on its remaining Reserve. Suspension of the Bank Act, permitting the total note issue to be increased, would make it possible to satisfy the public's abnormal desire for liquid reserves, and thus to restore commercial confidence.

Obviously, there is nothing inflationary about an emergency increase in the fiduciary issue to allay a *crise de confiance.* It merely prevents a sharp deflation of credit (and of the national income) in precisely the same way as the neutralization, in less exceptional circumstances, of a seasonal or other temporary increase in the demand for currency. The matter would be very different with a suspension made necessary by a steady and continuing drain, whether external or internal. Even if the drain were internal, a persistently rising demand for currency would almost certainly be associated with an expansion in the volume of internal transactions, and beyond a certain point with all the other phenomena of an inflation.

What action can the central bank take to arrest such a drain before the Reserve has fallen to danger point? The obvious course, seemingly, would be for the Bank simply to refrain from neutralizing completely the efflux of currency. Surely, one might argue, this would reduce bank cash and promote a multiple contraction of bank deposits, which in turn would depress the level of business activity and therefore of incomes, so reducing the demand for currency? But in fact the Bank could not, except in the very short period, significantly reduce its total assets, and therefore bank cash, simply by allowing notes to run out without taking any other action whatever.

Such reasoning from elementary arithmetic leaves out of account one quite fundamental element in the situation. It is that the initial contraction in bank cash would necessarily cause short-term interest rates to rise. A rise in interest rates is, of course, the invariable response in a free market to any shortage of liquid funds. When money is tight, borrowers become more

1. See Chapter VI.

ardent in their demands and lenders more coy about satisfying them, securities are offered for sale and buyers are less forthcoming. If the initial stringency is confined to bank cash, and not yet communicated to the rest of the system by a contraction in bank deposits, the resulting rise in interest rates will occur mainly in the short-term market. To protect their cash reserves, the banks will be less willing to buy bills or to lend at short-term to the discount market, and may even call in outstanding money-market loans. The discount market, in turn, will be less willing and able to buy bills. Money and bill rates will rise. But such a rise could not go very far without it becoming more profitable for the discount market to borrow from the Bank of England than from the commercial banks. If the stringency is severe, the market will in fact be 'driven into the Bank' to raise funds with which to repay their former borrowings from the commercial banks. As we have seen, the Bank cannot in practice refuse to make such advances, and at any moment there is a fixed rate at which it will do so, namely, Bank Rate.[1] As soon as market rates were driven up to equality with Bank Rate, therefore, the initial reduction in the Banking Department's assets would be reversed by an increase in discounts and advances, with an accompanying increase in bankers' deposits.

Precisely this mechanism was, in fact, regularly invoked before the war for the very purpose of expanding bank cash reserves over the turn of the year and half-year, when the commercial banks make up their accounts all on the same day. At these times, the technique of 'window-dressing'[2] could not be practised, and additional central bank credit would be needed to permit the banks to show the conventional ratio of cash to deposits. These routine seasonal demands the Bank was, of course, prepared to satisfy, since it was known that the demand for additional bank cash would be temporary. Other things equal, it could be taken for granted that once the critical date was passed market rates would promptly fall below Bank Rate again, and the market would therefore have every inducement

1. The accommodation may take two forms: the discounting of eligible paper or short-period loans against such paper.

2. See Chapter IX, pages 93–4.

to restrict its borrowings from the Bank to the unavoidable minimum.

If, on the other hand, the Bank wished to initiate a real contraction of credit, its obligations as lender of last resort would soon frustrate any attempt to do so if Bank Rate were not advanced when necessary so as to keep it permanently above the level of market rates. Starting from a position of credit abundance, with market rates well below the prevailing Bank Rate, open-market sales of assets will serve to mop up surplus credit and so drive up market rates to equality with Bank Rate. At that point their usefulness is exhausted, for any further open-market sales will promptly be offset by borrowings from the central bank *unless Bank Rate is raised.* In short, open-market operations (as a means of tightening credit, at least) are no more than an adjunct to Bank Rate, a means of rendering the prevailing Bank Rate 'effective'.

In the classical theory, then, it is the indirect weapon of Bank Rate changes, not the direct weapon of open-market sales, that is the real instrument for the enforcement of monetary policy. The tacit assumption is that there must be a limit to the advance in Bank Rate that will be needed, because at some stage the credit stringency will depress business activity and therefore reduce the *demand* both for commercial bank credit and for central bank credit.

Unfortunately, experience since 1955 throws some doubt upon the validity of this assumption under modern conditions, when the call money and discounts of the banks are mainly represented, not by commercial paper, but by Treasury bills. For, in addition to the discount market, there exists yet another customer whose importunities cannot in practice be refused: namely, the Government. In former days, if it became dearer to borrow in London than in other financial centres, bills would be switched elsewhere for discount and the liquid assets of the banks be reduced. There is no similar assurance that a rise in the Treasury bill rate will bring about a reduction in the supply of Treasury bills, nor, therefore, that a rise in Bank Rate will necessarily reduce bank deposits and the total liquid holdings of the public. Moreover, if the stock of money is not reduced and business confidence remains high, the rise in overdraft rates associated with a rise in Bank Rate may do little to deter even private borrowers.[1]

Under these conditions it appears that a more certain method of reducing bank deposits is for the Treasury to issue long-term securities to the public and to apply the proceeds in redemption of floating debt, particularly Treasury bills in the hands of the banking system and which provide the foundation on which the superstructure of bank deposits is erected; for if the banks are unwilling to allow their liquidity ratio to fall below a certain level (see Chapter VIII) this means that deposits cannot be more than a certain multiple of their liquid assets. The process of funding floating debt by issues of long-term securities, however, implies that the authorities must be willing, if need be, to put pressure on the gilt-edged market and allow the long-term rate of interest to rise. It follows that under present-day conditions the long-term rate of interest is potentially a more effective instrument of monetary control than the short-term rate, though Bank Rate still has its uses.

1. For a fuller exposition of these questions see 'The Floating Debt Problem,' *Lloyds Bank Review*, April 1956, and also *The Banker*, April 1956, *et seq.*

CHAPTER V

BILLS AND THE BILL MARKET

RECURRENT references in previous chapters will have made it plain that the London discount market has traditionally played an important rôle in our monetary system. We must now deal more explicitly with the organization and functions of the discount market, which in turn calls for some preliminary explanation of the bill of exchange. That emphatically does not imply that the term discount market is synonymous with bill market. Nowadays, a large part of the market's earnings is derived from holding and dealing in short-dated Government bonds. Admittedly, these bond operations are ultimately possible only because the discount market is at the same time a bill market; but even in this aspect of its activities the commercial bill now occupies a very minor place compared with the Treasury bill.

The bill of exchange is, of course, a credit instrument of great antiquity, and until the war of 1914 its functions as one of the main instruments of short-term lending, as the staple commodity handled by the discount market and as one of the main assets of the commercial banks, endowed it with great monetary significance. Even in eclipse, the bill of exchange is still of importance in the world of commerce, but its former place in the monetary system has been almost wholly usurped by the Treasury bill. Nevertheless, it is worth while to be clear about the basic features of a commercial bill transaction, for only thus can we understand how such financial institutions as the accepting houses and the discount market came to develop their special functions.

The bill of exchange, then, is a genus of many species, one of them the everyday cheque, which is a bill of exchange payable on demand drawn on a banker. Hence the man in the street can most readily envisage a typical commercial bill of exchange as a 'cheque' drawn, not by a customer on his bank, but by one trader on another who owes him money (e.g., in respect of goods purchased), requiring the latter to pay the debt either on demand or at some definite future date (e.g., 'ninety days after sight'). The debtor 'accepts' the bill – that is, acknowledges the debt and pledges himself to pay the bill at maturity – by putting his signature on it.[1] Having done so, he has until the maturity date to dispose of the goods and so put himself in a position to pay the bill at maturity.

What gave the bill of exchange its special importance, however, was the fact that the supplier of the goods need not wait until the bill matures before reimbursing himself for the goods. As soon as the bill is accepted, he can sell it – naturally for something less than its face value – to somebody else possessing idle cash to invest for a short period; for the acceptor is pledged to pay the debt acknowledged in the bill, not to the original creditor alone but to *any* bona fide holder presenting the bill at maturity. Moreover, any person purchasing the bill in good faith, even from a party whose title to the bill was defective, will himself establish an impregnable title to it. It is this fact which constitutes the characteristic of 'negotiability' (shared also by, for example, bank notes) that made the bill of exchange such an excellent short-term investment for banks and others. The bill of exchange is *par excellence* an assignable debt; and we saw at the outset that certain kinds of assignable debts – i.e., bank notes and bank deposits – are today the chief forms of money.

It has been said that the holder of a bill wishing to obtain cash for it at once instead of waiting until the bill matures can sell, or as it is called 'discount', the bill. Naturally, the rate of discount (the rate at which interest is *deducted* from the face amount of the bill) will vary with, among other things, the credit standing of the parties to it. This opens the way for cer-

1. Or getting an acceptance house to do so – see p. 49.

tain kinds of specialization, as may be seen from the diagram below.

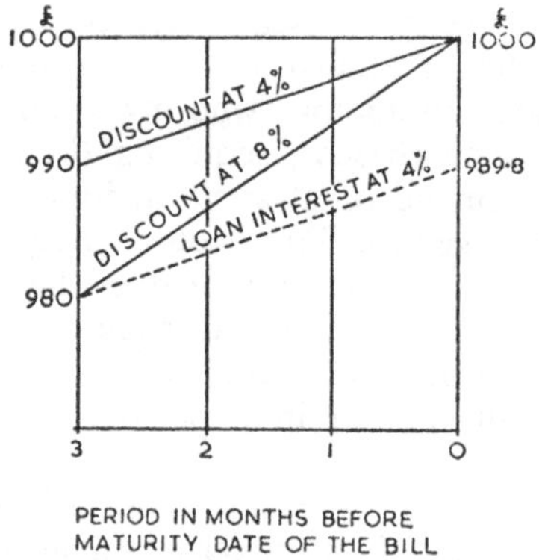

Diagram 2

On the vertical axis we measure amounts in money, on the horizontal axis the passage of time, starting on the left-hand side at a point three months before the maturity date of the bill, which is represented by the right-hand line. Let us suppose that the bill is drawn for a face amount of £1,000 and is at once offered for discount. If the appropriate discount rate is 4 per cent the market price of the bill will be approximately £990 (i.e., £1,000 less three months' discount at an annual rate of 4 per cent). Thereafter, the value of the bill will steadily rise – as shown by the sloping line – until it reaches £1,000 at the maturity date. After one month it will be worth £993⅓, after two months £996⅔, and so on. Both these points, like all the other points corresponding to the value of the bill at any time during its life, lie on the straight line connecting £990 on the left of the diagram with £1,000 on the right-hand side.[1] If, on the other hand, the appropriate discount rate is 8 per cent, the initial market value of the bill will be only about £980, and the

1. This is an approximation. Allowing for the element of compound interest, the line would not be straight but very slightly convex downwards, since at first the daily appreciation represents interest on only £990, while just before maturity it represents interest on nearly £1,000. In practice, however, a short-dated bill will normally command a lower *rate* than a full-dated bill, in which case the curve becomes concave downwards.

subsequent appreciation will be traced out by the straight line connecting this point with £1,000.

Now let us suppose that a bill drawn on a small trader of poor commercial standing would command a discount rate no better than 8 per cent, whereas a bill on a first-class merchant house of undoubted repute could be discounted at 4 per cent. (So wide a margin between the rates is probably quite unrealistic, but that does not affect the principle involved.) It follows that if the merchant house could be induced to step into the shoes of the small trader and accept the bill, the seller of the bill could afford to pay a commission of anything less than £10 and still be better off. This was the origin of the accepting houses, originally merchant firms whose high standing enabled their acceptances to be placed at a very 'fine' (i.e., low) rate. They were thus able to earn substantial commissions by lending their name to other traders, and came gradually to specialize in this and other financial functions while abandoning their own trading activities.

In addition to a high credit standing an accepting house clearly requires a good judgment of credit risks, since in lending its name it guarantees payment of the bill at maturity. In other words, the acceptance commission is largely a payment for risk-bearing. It need not be said that pressure of competition would tend always to limit the size of acceptance commissions, so that traders utilizing an acceptance credit would obtain their accommodation far more cheaply than by discounting their own bills. In 1957, a typical acceptance commission would be about 1¼ per cent per annum.

Two other forms of specialization help to explain the functions of the discount market. It is apparent from the diagram that the purchase of a bill at a high discount rate and its re-sale at a lower rate will yield a profit. The opportunities of doing this might occur, for example, through a fall in Bank Rate after the purchase of the bill. As it nears maturity, in any case, a bill normally commands a slightly lower rate than when it has several months to run to maturity. To take a purely hypothetical example in order to illustrate the arithmetic of the matter, if a full three months bill were discounted at 8 per cent and resold on the same day at 4 per cent, this would yield a profit of £10, less expenses. If the purchaser had to wait a month before rediscounting the bill at 4 per cent, the operation would yield a total gross profit of £13⅓, of which about half may be regarded as interest on £980 for one month at 8 per cent per annum, and the remaining half as a 'jobbing profit' reflecting the margin between the buying and selling rates (on the diagram, the distance between the 8 per cent and 4 per cent lines where these intersect with the vertical representing two months before maturity of the bill). If the resale took place after two months, the total profit would be £16⅔.

One of the main functions of the bill market in its heyday was to buy bills from traders wishing to obtain ready cash and sell them, under discount at a slightly lower rate, to bankers and others with liquid funds to invest for a short period.[1] The sellers of bills and the ultimate buyers of them found it worth while to pay this 'turn in the rate' for the same reasons that it pays the community to employ intermediaries – agents, wholesalers, retailers – in any other capacity. For the banker the main advantages were (1), that he obtained bills which had already passed under the scrutiny of an expert in the assessment of credit risks and (2), that from its substantial and assorted portfolios the market could usually supply him with bills maturing on the particular dates when the banker wished to be supplied with cash to meet anticipated demands.

The drawback was that once he had bought the bill the banker, unlike any other holder, would be compelled to wait until the maturity date before he could turn it into cash again; for – in peace-time, at any rate – convention precluded a bank from re-selling a bill which had once found shelter in its portfolio. Until its maturity date, in other words, the bill would represent in practice an irrevocable lock-up of funds, detracting somewhat from its other advantages as a banking asset.

Fortunately, a banking asset so safe and so readily realizable as to be almost the equivalent of actual cash was made available by the second of the two main kinds of specialization which explain the growth of the discount market. That asset is 'call

1. If the bill dealer endorsed the bills and so guaranteed their being met at maturity, the 'turn in the rate' would in part represent payment for lending his name in this way, on all fours with an acceptance commission.

money', meaning loans to the discount market (and to a less extent to the Stock Exchange), repayable on demand or at very short notice. Instead of using their liquid funds to buy bills the banks can lend these funds at short notice to the discount market, which invests them in bills bought on its own account. Provided the rate charged on the loans is below the discount rate for bills the operation will yield the market a profit. For example, if the discount house borrows from a bank at 4 per cent, in order to buy a bill which it discounts at 8 per cent; the operation, if the bill is held to maturity, will yield a profit of just over £10 (see diagram). Such a profit is known as a 'running profit' because it is produced by holding bills against borrowed money and not by re-selling them. While the margin between money rates and bill rates may sometimes be small, it must be remembered that the market runs bills against borrowed money to the extent of many times its own resources.

Like any other profit under competitive conditions, however, the running profit on bills is obtained only by incurring a risk. In this instance the chief risk is that the bank might call in its loan before the maturity date of the bills in which the loan had been invested by the discount house. If only one or two of the banks were calling in loans, the market could hope to replace them by borrowing from other banks with cash to lend – thus incidentally making the available bank cash go as far as possible and acting in the most literal sense as a money market. By offering a return on any idle funds available for investment, even for a very short period, the discount market in effect canalized them into a single reservoir of short-term credit and ensured the active employment of the whole of this fund. If, on the other hand, the banks *as a whole* should be calling in loans at any particular time, it follows that there is only one quarter to which the market could look as a buyer of bills or a source of fresh loans with which to repay the commercial banks. That source is, of course, the Bank of England, fulfilling its function as lender of last resort.

In the second half of the nineteenth century it became accepted doctrine that the Bank would never refuse to buy or lend against eligible bills (short-dated bills of good quality), so that the market was not exposed to the risk of being actually unable to repay the banks on demand. If it were forced 'into the Bank', however, the market received its accommodation at not less than Bank Rate, which we have already seen would always be higher than the market rate for bills and *a fortiori* higher than call money rates. For the period of its borrowings from the Bank of England, in other words, the market's running profit would be converted into a loss. Should Bank Rate itself be raised, of course, the loss would be magnified, though in the opposite case of a reduction in Bank Rate the market would stand to make a windfall gain.

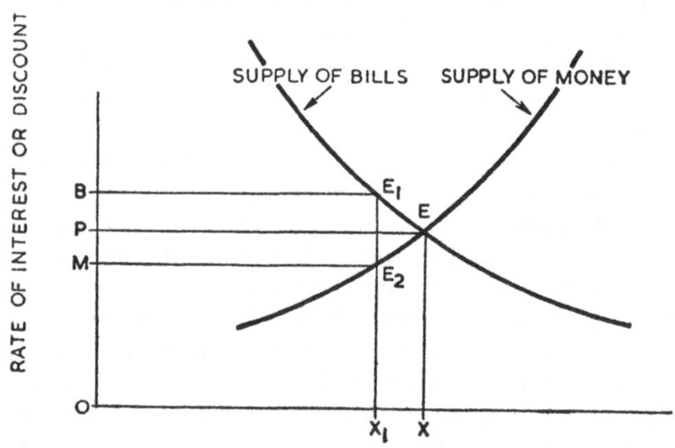

Diagram 3

E represents position of equilibrium if owners of loanable funds buy bills direct from their holders; the turnover in the market is OX, and OP represents both money rate and bill rate. E_1 and E_2 show position of equilibrium if owners of loanable funds deal through intermediaries, i.e., the discount market. The turnover in the market is OX_1, the money rate OM, and the bill rate OB. Given competitive conditions, E_1E_2 will represent the narrowest margin between money and bill rates needed to compensate the bill brokers for their services. Alternatively, E_1 and E_2 may be regarded as the equilibrium points in *two* distinct markets – for bills and money respectively – as shown in the next diagram:

Diagrams 3 and 4 represent in terms of the conventional demand and supply curves the inter-relationship between bill rates and money rates under conditions of pure competition. Inpractice, call money rates charged by the clearing banks are now fixed at a definite level in relation to Bank Rate, and normally move only when Bank Rate is changed. The call money rate, is, in fact, only one of a whole complex of short-term rates which are geared to Bank Rate in this way. The most direct link is that between Bank Rate and the London deposit rate (i.e., the rate allowed by the banks on their customers' balances held in deposit accounts as distinct from current accounts). Except in times of very cheap money, when Bank Rate itself may be no higher than 2 per cent, deposit rate is usually fixed

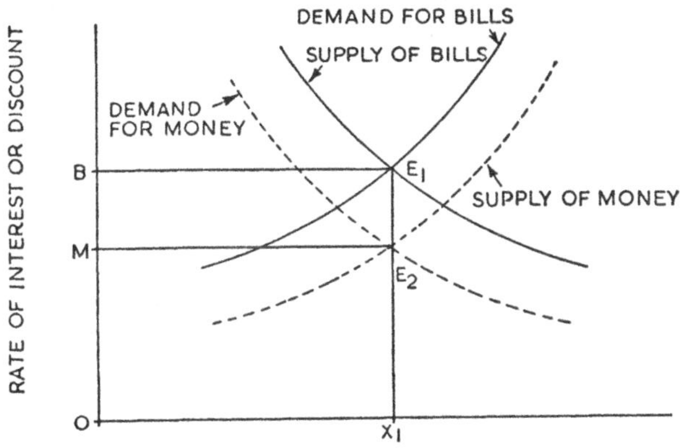

Diagram 4

An increase in the supply of loanable funds represents a shift to the right in the supply curve for money and the demand curve for bills, producing a new position of equilibrium to the right of OX_1 (i.e., with a larger turnover) with a decline in both money and bill rates. Similarly, an increase in the supply of bills represents a shift to the right both in the supply curve for bills and the demand curve for money, producing a new equilibrium, also with a larger turnover, but with higher money and bill rates; and so on.

at 2 per cent below Bank Rate. But the rates which the banks charge for loans must clearly bear some relation to the rates which they themselves pay for money, so that overdraft rates, as well as deposit rate, also move with Bank Rate. For various categories of borrowers, overdraft rates may be ½ per cent, 1 per cent or 1½ per cent over Bank Rate, with a minimum of 4 or 5 per cent.

For many years, the rate for clearing bank call money also varied only with changes in Bank Rate, the level being fixed somewhat higher than deposit rate, with at times a slightly higher rate for loans secured by bonds than for loans against bills. Since the reduction in Bank Rate from 5½ to 5 per cent in February 1957 the same rate has been fixed for bond money as for bill money, but this rate applies only to so-called 'regular' money, the rate for the remainder varying with the state of the market (i.e., in sympathy with the fluctuating rate for non-clearing bank money).

CHAPTER VI

PHASES IN DISCOUNT MARKET EVOLUTION

It has already been stressed that the term 'discount market' is no longer synonymous with 'bill market', that the market's rôle in our modern economy derives at least as much from its operations in short-term bonds, which for a generation past have furnished the bulk of its earnings. This shift of emphasis from bills to bonds is only one among many changes of function which have punctuated the history of the market since the industrial revolution. Time and again structural changes in methods of finance or in the credit machinery have threatened to render the market less important, if not wholly redundant, and each time the market's survival as an integral part of the financial mechanism has been assured by the assumption of new functions. In short, the discount market has had as many lives as a cat, and our purpose in this chapter is to give a very brief outline of some of the chief phases in its development.

Though the origins of the market go back to the goldsmiths and the use of the bill of exchange as a means of remittance, we need go no farther back for our purposes than the early stages of the industrial revolution; on the other hand, we shall return to review the more recent developments in greater detail after discussing the assets structure of the clearing banks.

(1) Our first phase, then, covers the early decades of the nineteenth century. This was an era of poor communications and small local banks, before the development of the present countrywide networks of branch banking. In this phase the most important function of the London brokers was to collect the bills sent in from the industrial areas, which needed working capital to finance their expanding trade, and sell them to banks

in the rich agricultural areas, such as East Anglia, where most of the savings of the country originated. The market thus acted as an intermediary between the agricultural saver and the industrial borrower, in the process of providing the banks in the agricultural regions with a medium for the investment of their accumulating deposits.

(2) In the second phase – the later decades of the century – this function was largely destroyed by the development of branch banking. Henceforth the transfer of savings from the agricultural to the industrial areas takes place to an increasing extent inside the bank network; though the bill of exchange remains an important instrument for the finance of inland trade, the larger banking units often lend direct to their customers in industrial areas the deposits received from customers of the rural branches. Meanwhile, however, the London market had come to render important services to the banks. In addition to supplying the banks with selected bills of the desired maturities, it provided an outlet for call money. As we have seen, this is intrinsically superior, as a banking asset, to a direct purchase of bills because (a) the lending banker is no longer concerned with changes in the capital value of the bills, whether due to a rise in interest rates or non-payment at maturity; (b) the call loan has no fixed maturity but can be called in at any time; and (c) it therefore permits indirect access to Bank of England credit.

This development of the call loan was of fundamental importance in the shaping of the British banking system, and accounts for some of its most characteristic features. In most other countries the commercial banks are accustomed to rediscount bills or obtain accommodation direct from the central bank in some other form when they are pressed for cash. The British system has developed differently.[1] Thanks to the call loan system, however, the banks lost nothing through the severance of direct relations with the central bank. Call money became fully as effective a second-line reserve as rediscountable bills. Indeed, the interposition of the discount market between the commercial banks and the central bank created a mechanism

1. For the origins of the conventional ban on bank rediscounting see W. T. C. King, *History of the London Discount Market*.

of credit regulation far more sensitive than the normal method of direct rediscounts. Under the latter system, it may often happen that one or more of the commercial banks is borrowing from the central institution, while others have surplus reserves. In the British system the discount market acts *inter alia* as a mechanism for the clearing of day-to-day surpluses of funds between the banks. This means, first, that there need be no recourse to the central bank until the whole of the existing central bank credit has been fully utilized, and, secondly, that any measures taken by the central bank to tighten or relax credit will be disseminated at once throughout the system as a whole.

(3) In the last quarter of the nineteenth century the use of the bill of exchange for the finance of domestic trade (the 'inland bill') suffered a decline. For this the chief reasons seem to have been, first, that many traders came to dislike seeing their names circulating in the open market as borrowers on bills and, secondly, that they grew to prefer the greater elasticity of the bank overdraft compared with the inflexible maturity date of a bill, the slightest delay in meeting which would wreak havoc with the defaulter's credit standing. In the meantime, however, the growth of the accepting houses and the stability of the pound sterling under the gold standard (or, if you prefer, of gold under the sterling standard) led to the world-wide use of the sterling bill for the finance not only of Britain's own external trade but of many movements of goods which never came within thousands of miles of these shores.

This world-wide resort to London credits, moreover, was achieved with little or no strain on this country's savings; for the pre-eminence of London as an international banking centre fostered the habit the world over of sending short-term funds to London for employment. In part, such funds were lodged on deposit with the discount houses, who would use them to finance overseas sterling credits. Thus the market became, among other things, 'an intricate mechanism for the conversion of foreign short-term money into foreign-drawn bills'.[1]

As a result, it came to occupy a key rôle in the British financial mechanism. We have already seen that under gold standard

1. See the series of special articles on the discount market in *The Banker*, December 1934.

conditions the drain on the Banking Department's gold reserve resulting from an adverse balance of payments would almost automatically set in train a contraction of credit, which could be enforced only by a rise in Bank Rate and therefore of short-term interest rates in general. In the last analysis, higher interest rates will correct the disequilibrium only if they serve eventually to bring about a contraction in money incomes in relation to those of the outside world. Through the medium of the discount market, however, the rise in rates would help at once to stem the drain by inducing appropriate movements of short-term capital. Discount rates having risen, London will now be a less attractive centre in which to borrow. The volume of new credits opened will fall short of the volume of sterling bills falling due for payment, so that on balance overseas borrowers will have to remit funds to London to meet their maturing obligations. At the same time the higher yields now obtainable will tempt overseas banks and other owners of liquid funds to send balances to London on deposit or increase their purchases of sterling bills. The latter movement represents the celebrated 'Continental investment demand' for sterling bills, which figured so prominently in gold standard literature and remained active until the shock of the 1931 depreciation. The higher rates obtainable on deposits lodged with the discount houses or banks would also serve to attract funds from abroad.[1]

Without the intervention of a single 'planner', in other words, a rise in Bank Rate would bring about a reduction in London's short-term lendings abroad and an increase in London's short-term borrowings just at the right time, setting up under both heads a demand for sterling for purposes of remittance and so checking the outflow of gold during the interval before the more fundamental adjustments initiated by the rise in Bank Rate could take effect. All this came about through the operations of the discount market; truly, 'it was during the days of specialization in international bills that the market reached the apex of its power and importance'.[2]

(4) Our fourth phase covers the period from 1918 to the out-

1. Provided the rise in interest rates was not offset by a widening of the forward discount on sterling – see Einzig, *Forward Exchange*.

2. Paul Bareau, *The Banker*, December 1934.

set of the world depression and the devaluation of sterling in September 1931. For the discount market this appears in retrospect little more than a period of painless transition to the very different phase which followed. After the restoration of the gold standard in 1925, especially, it might have appeared for a time that the war of 1914–18 had brought no very radical changes. International trade struggled back to something like normality and the London acceptance credit easily held its own in face of the ineffective rivalry of New York and Paris. Hence the market retained its basic functions of the pre-1914 era, but it was learning others which were to prove its salvation after the collapse of international trade in the early 'thirties, with the virtual disappearance of the international bill of exchange.

The fundamental change brought to the City by the 1914–18 war was that, *for the first time, Government paper came to predominate over commercial paper*. In particular, that war brought the rise of the Treasury bill, a short-term Government promissory note invented by Walter Bagehot expressly in imitation of the commercial bill of exchange.[1] Before 1914 the issue of Treasury bills rarely exceeded £30 millions; in 1921 it touched a peak (until the 1939 war) of £1,200 millions, and during most of the 'twenties fluctuated around £600 millions.

For a time, dealings in Treasury bills were actually highly profitable, so much so that they helped to attract new entrants and capital to the market. Nevertheless, the substitution of the Treasury bill for the commercial bill as the main stock-in-trade of the market represented a certain deterioration in the functions of the discount market: for the discount broker in the heyday of the market was essentially an expert in the assessment and fine grading of credit risks, and no nice discrimination is required in the selection of Treasury bills, even though tendering for Treasuries did call for a certain *expertise* in such matters as choice of maturity dates. Secondly, the rise of the Treasury bill tended to diminish somewhat the advantages to the banks of a call loan as compared with a direct purchase of bills, since the credit even of the strongest discount house can scarcely add to that of the British Government.

The war-time deficits responsible for the great expansion in

1. See next chapter.

the Treasury bill issue also brought a considerable increase in the outstanding volume of short-dated Government bonds, constantly replenished as successive issues approached maturity and became eligible in their turn as money-market 'shorts'. This provided ample opportunities for jobbing profits, but at first market portfolios of bonds held on borrowed money remained on a modest scale, since market operations in bonds were still regarded with distaste by the purists. The reason for this disapproval, of course, was that a bond having a life of anything up to five years, as contrasted with the maximum three months of a typical bill, would decline far more drastically in value should interest rates rise, and, moreover, could not normally be pledged with or sold to the Bank of England should a stringency develop.[1] At the worst, the depreciation could not only wipe out the borrower's margin but produce losses that might lead to default on the loan. If in spite of this unpleasant possibility call loans secured by bonds were to qualify as a suitable banking asset, it was clearly important that the borrowing institution should possess substantial free reserves; and it was precisely that condition that was not always fulfilled by the discount market of the 'twenties, which included a number of small and relatively weak units. That problem, however, only assumed real importance with the great expansion in bond operations during the cheap money era of the 'thirties, which constitutes the next clearly-defined phase in the market's history.

(5) In due course we shall examine in some detail the management of interest rates. For the present, suffice it to say that the cheap money era was ushered in with the reduction of Bank Rate to 2 per cent in June 1932 as an adjunct to the great conversion of some £2,000 millions of War Loan from a 5 per cent to a 3½ per cent basis. At that level Bank Rate remained for the unprecedented period of over nineteen years, save for a brief

1. A short-dated bond necessarily fluctuates in value far more than a bill with only a few weeks to run, but far less than a long-dated or irredeemable bond. If market yields should rise from 2½ per cent to 5 per cent, then 2½ per cent Consols (redeemable only at par) will fall from 100 to 50. On the other hand, a 2½ per cent bond maturing in 5 years will show a gross yield to redemption (ignoring compound interest) of 5 per cent if the price falls only to 87½, while a three months bill will show a yield of 5 per cent at about 98¾ per cent of the face value.

and quite pointless increase (to 4 per cent) at the outbreak of war in September 1939, reversed after a few weeks. For the discount market, the early years of cheap money were a period of important structural changes. The most tangible evidence of the changed conditions is to be seen in the increased concentration on dealings in bonds, which during the 'twenties seldom exceeded much more than a sixth of the total assets of the principal houses,[1] but in the early 'thirties came to represent about a third of their balance sheet totals. Two chief factors impelled the market into this increased reliance on bond operations. The positive motive was, of course, provided by the exceptionally profitable market conditions created by the fall in interest rates and therefore in security yields, with a resulting appreciation in the market value even of the short-dated bonds dealt in by the market. Even so, the prospect of jobbing profits on a rising market might not have proved such an irresistible attraction had it not been reinforced by the negative stimulus of the exceptionally unprofitable state of bill dealings.

This resulted from a persistent shortage of bills in relation to the demand for them. On the side of supply the dearth was due to two main factors: (1) the depression in international trade reduced the supply of commercial paper to a mere third or quarter of its former volume; (2) the authorities, as we shall see in greater detail later on, were unwilling to allow the Treasury bill issue to rise above an arbitrary limit of under £1,000 millions, although the influx of short-term capital into this country was creating a greatly increased demand for Treasury bills and other liquid assets on the part of the overseas owners of sterling funds, so that the volume of tender Treasury bills available to the domestic banks was continuously depleted. At the same time, the demand for money market assets on the part of the clearing banks, as will also be explained more fully later on, was increased by the expansion in bank cash and deposits in connection with the cheap money policy of those years.

Throughout the 'thirties, in consequence, the margin between money and bill rates remained infinitesimal and at one

1. The three discount houses then registered as public companies, namely, Alexanders, National, and Union Discount.

time actually became negative. Such conditions threatened the very existence of the discount market, and in 1934 and 1935 a number of measures were taken, by the market or the banks, to create more favourable operating conditions. They included the following:

(i) The clearing banks reduced their rate for call loans against bill collateral from 1 per cent to ½ per cent, leaving the rate for bond money at 1 per cent. By implication this gave for the first time official recognition to the market's bond dealings.

(ii) The banks agreed not to buy or tender for bills at less than the bill money rate. This meant that the market could no longer make an actual loss on any bills resold to the banks and remedied the former illogical position by which the banks were sometimes prepared to lend for three months – through the purchase of a bill – at a lower rate than they were charging the market for overnight loans. By offering a certain, if small, profit on any bills the market might secure for resale, these arrangements led to a great increase in applications for bills. Market houses would tender for a larger quantity of bills than they expected either to secure or to be able to finance; indeed, there were many so-called 'stagging' applications for bills which the tenderers had no intention of taking up at all, but hoped to resell to the banks in advance as soon as they secured an allotment at the tender. To overcome this difficulty,

(iii) the market formed a syndicate, agreeing to tender at a uniform rate agreed in advance, and to limit their applications to a figure decided by reference to the resources of the various houses. Normally the syndicate tender would equal the total of bills on offer. Although it means that the tenders are no longer competitive (except with those of applicants outside the market) this system clearly has at least the tacit approval of the authorities. In addition,

(iv) the banks eventually agreed (a) not to tender for bills at all, but to fill their requirements exclusively by purchases through the market, and (b) not to buy 'hot' bills (i.e., not to buy any bill until at least a week after issue), thus eliminating the 'stag' by compelling all applicants to take up and finance their allotments for a minimum period of a week.

By mid-1935 these arrangements were successful in levering

up bill rates to a slight fraction over the bill money rate. Even so, bill operations returned only a negligible profit. The market, was forced progressively further into reliance on bond operations for its main earnings, a movement assisted by the rising trend of gilt-edged prices and by the 'legalization' of bond dealings through the fixing by the banks of a separate rate for call loans against bond collateral. Meanwhile, the Bank of England encouraged at suitable opportunities the consolidation of the market into stronger units with resources of at least £500,000, a minimum later raised to £1,000,000. The first wave of changes came in 1933, but thereafter the consolidation movement made little progress until 1938. On the eve of the war the number of market houses had been reduced from twenty-four to eighteen, but there had been little, if any, reduction in their combined resources.

(6) At one time it seemed that the traditional functions of the market might be further undermined by the new techniques of war finance. The war-time expansion of the public sector necessarily brought a sharp increase in the transfers of funds between bankers' deposits and public deposits, and consequently demanded a vigilant neutralization policy to prevent serious immobilizations of funds and dislocation of credit. In the early months of the war the authorities solved this problem by recourse to direct dealings in bills with the joint stock banks. Though not absolutely unknown before the war, such dealings do of course run counter to the normal conventions.[1] In June 1940 the Treasury bill itself was superseded as the primary instrument of deficit finance by the Treasury deposit receipt, which did not disappear again until February 1952. In most respects, T.D.R.s might be regarded (see pages 155–6) as equivalent to a six months' Treasury bill. From the discount market point of view, however, there was the important difference that deposit receipts were issued direct to the banks by the authori-

1. Though not seriously so, since any purchases of bills from the commercial banks take place on the initiative of the authorities and hence cannot be construed as a sign of weakness on the part of the banks. To ease credit, for example, the authorities purchase short-dated maturities from the clearing banks which promptly replace these by purchases of longer-dated bills from the market. It is thus the latter which receives the benefit of the additional funds.

ties and were not transferable. Despite the sweeping war-time expansion in bank deposits and therefore in bank assets as a whole, the money market assets of the banks at times actually fell below the pre-war level; the counterpart of the additional deposits was throughout provided mainly by Treasury deposit receipt holdings.

In the early post-war years the discount market played an important part in absorbing offerings of short-dated bonds sold by industrial companies to finance reconversion, and a series of increases in the capital of the market was approved by the Capital Issues Committee to enable it to perform this special function.

Since the return to more flexible monetary policies in 1951, dealings in bills have again become an important source of revenue to the market. Though temporarily reduced by the £1,000 millions funding operation of October 1951, the supply of Treasury bills has been more than adequate, while the margin between money rates and bill rates – for many years infinitesimal – has at times exceeded 1 per cent. On the other hand, the decline in gilt-edged prices associated with 'credit squeezes' and drastic increases in Bank Rate brought heavy losses on bond portfolios.

To sum up, we can say that the discount market remains an integral part of our financial mechanism, but an important part of its functions is now associated with operations in bonds as well as in bills.

CHAPTER VII

'TAP' AND 'TENDER'

IN 1876 a high official of the Treasury consulted Walter Bagehot on the question of devising a more satisfactory instrument of short-term Government borrowing than the old Exchequer bill. Bagehot advised that the best results would be obtained from a promissory note resembling as closely as possible the ordinary commercial bill, the ideal banking asset. The outcome was the Treasury bill, which remained the chief instrument of short-term Government borrowing until the 1939 war, when its supremacy was challenged for a number of years by the Treasury deposit receipt. Treasury bills were originally designed to cover temporary deficits in the national revenue in relation to current expenditure (see diagram on p. 66).

The Treasury bill issue outstanding at any time falls into two portions, 'tender' bills and 'tap' bills. Technically, these terms describe the method of issue, but the important distinction is that 'tender' bills are in effect receipts given by the Treasury for money borrowed from the *public* in the widest sense, while until the 1939 war 'tap' bills were issued exclusively to Government departments and agencies,[1] normally in respect of surplus funds lent at short-term to the Exchequer. Tender bills thus formed part of the *effective* floating debt (i.e., that held by the public), whereas tap bills issued to Government departments were little more than *nominal* debt, representing no more than an internal book-keeping transaction within the Government sector which might almost equally well have been accomplished by a mere entry in a ledger.

1. In 1941, tap bills were made available also to certain overseas central banks who were accumulating large sterling balances as a result of war finance, so that the former distinction between tap and tender bills became blurred.

SEASONAL PATTERN OF TENDER TREASURY BILL ISSUE

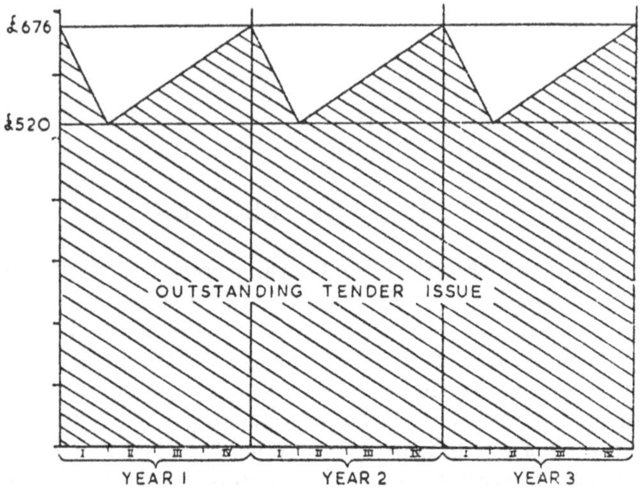

Diagram 5

The revenue inflow, even with P.A.Y.E., shows a marked seasonal pattern which tends to be reflected in the trend of the tender Treasury bill issue. Let us suppose that the budget is exactly balanced at a figure of £1,040 millions, with expenditure stable at a rate of £260 millions per quarter, but 40 per cent of the revenue accruing during the January-March quarter and 20 per cent in each of the other three quarters. If the April-December shortfall is financed entirely by Treasury bill borrowing, the outstanding tender issue on April 1 being £520 millions, the fluctuations in the issue will be as shown in the diagram.

Let us assume that in each of the first thirteen weeks of the year £40 millions of bills are allotted. At the last tender in March (i.e., that relating to bills to be issued from the beginning of April), the weekly offer must be raised to £44 millions, at the beginning of July to £48 millions, and at the beginning of October to £52 millions, reverting to £40 millions at the beginning of January.

It is, nevertheless, vital to remember that for financial purposes the Government sector is sharply divided into two parts: the central Exchequer and the Departments, which borrow from, and lend money to, the Exchequer. When the latter lend to the Exchequer, their loans are either placed on record as Ways and Means advances, or they are given acknowledgments of debt in the form of tap Treasury bills. Both of these figure in the floating debt, which in turn forms part of the national debt. This is often confusing to the layman, who tends to assume that if money is flowing in to public departments the national debt must be reduced. What happens, as we shall see, is that the Treasury does indeed use these funds to pay off *effective* debt held by the public or the banking system; but it has incurred liabilities to repay the Departments at some future time, so that the total national debt is shown as unchanged. A clear understanding of the distinction between the Exchequer and the Departments, and therefore of the 'scissors movements' between tap and tender bills, is the key to some of the most confusing aspects of our monetary system.

The so-called 'tap' bills are at all times available 'on tap' or 'through the tap' to Government departments or other eligible holders with surplus funds to invest, whereas a discount house or any other member of 'the public' wishing to buy newly-issued Treasury bills can obtain these only by application at the Friday tenders, when bills to a stated maximum amount to be issued during the succeeding week are offered to the highest bidders.

For many years, tender bills were issued only in three-months maturities, having an effective life which varied slightly according to the accident of the calendar; since 1956, this has been standardized at ninety-one days. In the final weeks of the calendar year, sixty-three day bills have also been offered since 1955. Bills are drawn for denominations of £5,000 and £10,000, but tenders must be for a minimum amount of £50,000. Bids are expressed as the amount offered per £100 of the face value, e.g., a bid of £99 15s. for a ninety-one day bill means a rate of discount of about 1 per cent per annum. Usually the market receives only a percentage of its applications at the 'syndicated'[1] rate, the remainder being allotted to outside bidders offering a higher price, though on rare occasions the market has either 'missed the bills' altogether by bidding too low, or has tendered at more than the 'bull's-eye' figure.

In deciding upon its tender rate the market must have regard to three main factors:

1. See p. 62.

(1) The maturity date of the bill, i.e., whether the day on which the holder of the bill will receive his money back is one on which money is likely to be in keen demand or the reverse. Until the end of 1946, when the practice of 'window-dressing' (see p. 93) was abandoned, by far the most sought-after maturity was December 31st, with June 30th a good second; for it was on those dates that all the banks *simultaneously* drew up their year-end or half-yearly statements and wished to show a conventional minimum cash ratio – 10 per cent – well above the actual cash ratio maintained by the banks *as a whole* at any other time of the year. From the beginning of 1947 the banks have sought to maintain at all times, and not only on make-up days, a ratio of 8 per cent, so that this particular distinction between different maturities has lost a great deal of its force.

(2) Prospective credit conditions during the succeeding week. In particular, will the banks be ready buyers of bills? – since bank purchases of bills already in market portfolios will release call money to enable the market to finance its allotment of the 'hot' (newly-issued) bills. Alternatively, will the banks be ready lenders of call money? Especially important is the prospective supply of 'outside' money, the rate for which fluctuates. Throughout the cheap money era, credit conditions were comfortable and, after 1939, even the normal year-end and end-June stringencies were 'ironed out' by official intervention. On occasion, however, tendering for bills – which means estimating credit conditions for ten days ahead – has involved a real credit risk. That was especially true, for example, during the Munich crisis and at the outbreak of war in 1939 but the market is confronted with similar problems whenever a rise in Bank Rate is imminent. Thus, on September 13th, 1957, with Bank Rate at 5 per cent, the market tendered for bills at an average rate of rather less than 4¼ per cent to find Bank Rate raised to 7 per cent in the following week.

A factor of special importance in prospective credit conditions is the question whether the volume of Treasury bills to be taken up during the succeeding week exceeds or falls short of the amount maturing, i.e., whether the week's Treasury bill operations will involve a net payment to the authorities, or conversely. What is significant is not the total *nominally* maturing during the week, but the amount still held by the market and the banks; for part of the maturing issues may meanwhile have passed into the hands of public departments or the Bank of England as the result of so-called 'special' purchases to ease credit conditions or, in recent years, as collateral for loans taken when the market has been forced 'into the Bank'.

(3) The volume of 'outside' competition for bills. The movements during the Munich crisis of 1938 will illustrate the importance of this factor. At the tender of August 26th, total applications for the £40 millions of bills on offer amounted to nearly £88 millions, and the market received 36 per cent of its applications. On September 16th, again with £40 millions of bills on offer, total applications dropped to below £56 millions, reflecting the decline in 'outside' applications, so that the market quota on an unchanged syndicate tender jumped to 66 per cent. Over long periods during the cheap money era, on the other hand, the high level of outside applications for bills was one factor tending to keep the bill rate down to an infinitesimal fraction over the cost of bill money.

By way of illustration, the table on page 70 summarizes the results of the tenders during three months of 1957, with a detailed statement of the results of the September 20th tender.

The table on page 71 summarizes the position of the floating debt as a whole during these months.

The total of tender bills outstanding at any date is not officially announced, but is obtained by adding together the amounts issued at the thirteen preceding tenders, making due allowance, of course, for any sixty-three day bills, issued during the period and already matured. Figures so obtained necessarily relate to Saturdays (when the whole of the bills allotted at the tender of the preceding week will have been issued and all those maturing during the week in question have been paid off). Totals for the tender issue are therefore not available for the end of quarters unless these happen to fall on a Saturday – a slight but avoidable inconvenience to the money market observer. Together with Ways and Means advances, tap bills constitute the floating assets of the public departments. It will be seen that the Bank of England also makes Ways and Means advances to the Treasury, but this form of finance is traditionally regarded as

TREASURY BILLS

Date of tender	Amount (£ million)			Three months' bills		
	Offered	Applied for	Allotted	Average rate of allotment		Allotted at max. rate*
				s.	d.	%
1956						
Sept. 21	280·0	280·0	280·0	103	4.86	55
1957						
June 21	250·0	394·6	250·0	77	1·35	59
,, 28	260·0	385·1	260·0	77	1·07	61
July 5	260·0	423·6	260·0	76	11·66	42
,, 12	250·0	424·8	250·0	76	11·24	36
,, 19	250·0	416·0	250·0	76	9·94	36
,, 26	230·0	396·2	230·0	76	10·82	32
Aug. 2	230·0	387·7	220·0	76	4·78	50
,, 9	220·0	375·9	210·0	77	7·48	32
,, 16	210·0	371·7	210·0	79	10·62	41
,, 23	220·0	363·1	220·0	81	0·81	51
,, 30	240·0	359·3	240·0	82	50·3	59
Sept. 6	250·0	399·8	250·0	84	5·06	38
,, 13	250·0	367·2	250·0	84	8·24	54
,, 20	250·0	347·9	250·0	132	1·02	63

* On September 20th tenders for 91 day bills at £98 7s. od. secured 51 per cent, higher tenders being allotted in full. The offering this week was for £270 million at 91 day bills.

---

* Acceptance of a tender at £98 7s. od. for a 91 day bill means that the applicant will earn £1 13s. od. in 91 days, or about £6 12s. 4½d. in 365 days. This is described as the rate of allotment; the percentage return on the £98 7s. od. invested in the bill is about 2s. 2½d. higher.

especially inflationary (because any increase in the total assets of the Banking Department tends to increase bank cash and therefore bank deposits) and is kept to a minimum.

The relationship between the tap and tender issues can be made clear only if we consider in broad outline the technique of Government finance as a whole. In the first place, there can be no increase in the national debt *as a whole* unless the dis-

FLOATING DEBT
(£ million)

Date	Treasury bills		Ways and Means advances		Total floating debt
	Tender	Tap	Public debt.	Bank of England	
1956					
Sept. 22	3,590·0	1,325·5	254·5	—	5,169·6
1957					
June 22	2,930·0	1,714·1	258·1	—	4,902·2
„ 30	4,681·9		259·7	—	4,941·6
July 6	2,940·0	1,746·4	248·3	3·3	4,937·9
„ 13	2,960·0	1,756·7	256·1	—	4,972·9
„ 20	2,980·0	1,784·9	242·7	0·5	5,008·1
„ 27	2,990·0	1,821·3	228·6	—	5,039·9
Aug. 3	3,020·0	1,771·8	229·0	0·8	5,021·6
„ 10	3,040·0	1,742·9	231·8	—	5,014·7
„ 17	3,050·0	1,752·2	290·3	1·0	5,093·5
„ 24	3,070·0	1,751·5	223·9	—	5,045·4
„ 31	3,070·0	1,758·6	235·9	1·3	5,065·7
Sept. 7	3,080·0	1,723·8	251·7	1·0	5,056·5
„ 14	3,090·0	1,763·0	232·3	—	5,085·3
„ 21	3,100·0	1,770·1	250·0	—	5,120·1

bursements of the *central* Government, both on current and capital account, exceed its current revenue, and conversely.

Let us suppose that at a particular moment the Treasury has a deficit. This can be met by borrowing from three main sources, corresponding to the three strata in our pyramid of credit:[1]

(i) *From the Bank of England.* Since the Bank is the Government's banker, this is the normal method of meeting any unforeseen financial requirements in the first instance. We have already seen that the Bank lends to the Government on Ways

1. We exclude external borrowing because for this purpose we are considering only operations requiring domestic finance. As such, externl borrowing enables the Government to *repay* an equivalent amount of internal debt, e.g., when the Government sells to the domestic public goods ar foreign exchange obtained by overseas borrowing, such as the American and Canadian loans of 1945.

and Means advances, and it may hold either tap or tender Treasury bills. Other things equal, such borrowing increases bank cash by an equivalent amount. If not avoided altogether, it should be confined, at least in peace-time, to covering purely temporary needs, the central bank advances being repaid at the earliest possible moment out of revenue or from the proceeds of borrowing through other channels. Indeed, it is a major objective of credit management to gauge correctly the Government's forthcoming receipts and payments, with the object of fixing the offer of Treasury bills at a level that will enable the Government to satisfy its requirements without the need for recourse to the central bank.

(ii) *From the commercial banks.* In a sense, borrowing from the commercial banks (whether directly or *via* the discount market) is deflationary in tendency in that such borrowing may be the means of 'mopping up' bank cash created by Government borrowings from the Bank of England. Let us suppose that bank cash, and therefore bank deposits, have been increased by £100 millions through such borrowings. All but £8 millions of the additional cash can be skimmed off by the sale of Treasury bills to the banks and/or the discount market, restoring the cash ratio to the normal 8 per cent. Unfortunately, this operation does nothing to reduce either bank deposits or the banks' total liquid assets. If as a result of these transactions the liquidity ratio rises substantially above the basic 30 per cent level, the banks will tend, other things equal, to add to their investments and perhaps to follow more liberal lending policies, in which case deposits will rise still further. This is, in fact, the normal process by which bank deposits are inflated under modern conditions.

(iii) *From the public* in the widest sense which includes, in addition to individuals and companies, financial institutions other than the banks and the discount market. The vitally important distinction between borrowing from the Bank of England or the commercial banks and borrowing from the public is that the latter will reduce, instead of expanding, bank deposits. The public is asked to surrender cash in exchange for securities, and this will tend to raise the long-term rate of interest, i.e., to depress gilt-edged prices. In general, borrowings from the public take the form of subscriptions to National Savings securities, purchases of tax reserve certificates and the proceeds of issues of marketable gilt-edged securities. Any deficit in excess of the total obtainable through these channels will require floating debt finance (unless, of course, funds are also flowing in to the Government sector in exchange for capital assets, e.g., the transfer of commodity stocks from public to private ownership, or the running down of gold and dollar reserves).

But in addition to borrowing from these three sources, the Government can also borrow what the ordinary man would regard as its 'own' money, namely, any currently accruing receipts of public departments. If the Departments invest in Treasury bills, such borrowings of their funds by the Exchequer will be reflected in an addition to the *tap* issue.[1] Naturally, the Departments may be accumulating surplus receipts at times when the Treasury has no need of floating debt finance. It nevertheless borrows the funds, issuing tap bills against them, and thus has actual cash in hand to be used for the repayment of *effective* debt held by the banks or the public. If it decides to pay off market bills (i.e., bills in the hands of the banks or the discount market), the increase in the tap issue will have its counterpart in a decline in the tender issue; the transaction as a whole will appear as a transfer of Treasury bills from the tender issue to the tap issue.[2]

The resulting contraction in the assets of the banks, however, will of course be matched by a contraction in their liabilities – that is, in bank deposits – for the Departmental surplus in question will consist of sums paid over to the department by

1. The Departments also hold special non-marketable medium or long-term securities issued to the National Debt Commissioners, usually, in repayment of these floating assets.

2. In practice, the reduction in the tender issue may follow the increase in tap issue with an appreciable time-lag. For example, if the Departmental surplus accrues on a Monday there will be no Treasury tender until the following Friday, when the total allotted can be reduced so that maturities will exceed issues during the following week. In the meantime, the surplus will take the form of cash held on public deposits with the Banking Department. To prevent this immobilization causing a stringency, however, the cash may be returned to the banks by means of a purchase of tender bills already in existence. The reduction in the *nominal* tender issue will not then take place until these bills in turn fall due for payment.

individuals drawing on their bank accounts. Any such reduction in the liquid assets of the public will tend to depress gilt-edged.[1] That can be avoided if the surplus is used to repay long-debt instead of floating debt which forms the counterpart of bank deposits. But the Government cannot repay long-term debt unless an issue happens to fall due for redemption or 'small savers'' securities are presented for encashment. The solution, if it is desired to prevent pressure on gilt-edged prices, is for the Departments not to invest their surplus in tap bills, but to use the funds to buy long-term debt hitherto held by the public. When this chain of transactions is complete, it is as though the public as a whole had paid over the sums due to the Departments by surrendering securities instead of cash, leaving the banking position completely unaffected. Actually, of course, the Departmental surplus will in fact be paid over in the first instance in the form of cash; but this cash will be returned to the system through the Departmental purchases of securities, reversing the initial impact on the banking position.

This acquisition of long-term securities by public departments is one of the strongest weapons at the disposal of the authorities for the management of the gilt-edged market, i.e., of the long-term rate of interest. For some years the receipts of the National Insurance Funds tended to exceed their disbursements, and this accumulating surplus provided a useful continuing source of support – or, rather, of potential support – for gilt-edged. It appears that the Issue Department of the Bank of England also holds long-term securities, so that the proceeds of any increase in the note issue are also potentially available to support the gilt-edged market.

The assistance rendered to the authorities is greatly enhanced by the wide latitude as to the *timing* of Departmental and extra-budgetary fund purchases of long-term securities. For a long period their accruing receipts may be invested in the liquid form of tap bills. If the Departments then exchange on a large scale out of tap bills into gilt-edged securities acquired from the public, this buying, compressed into a short period, may

1. Moreover, as we shall see in the next chapter, a funding of tender bills may impair the liquidity of the banks themselves and tend to produce a further contraction in deposits through 'pyramiding downwards'.

be the dominant influence on gilt-edged prices and yields. Hence, Departmental funds provide a formidable *masse de manoeuvre*, amounting now to several thousand millions of pounds.

During the period in which the Departmental surpluses are accruing and being invested in tap bills, the Treasury will be using these funds (unless they are needed to finance a current deficit) to pay off effective debt, probably floating debt held by the commercial banks, thus reducing bank deposits. If it is desired to support the gilt-edged market, the Department theoretically asks the Treasury to repay its tap bills; this the Treasury can do only with the proceeds of new borrowings from the banking system. The support afforded to the gilt-edged market derives from the expansion of bank credit by means of which the Departmental purchases are financed.

To take the main steps in a typical chain of transactions, we may suppose that at the outset a Department holds tap bills. It presents these for payment, and the Treasury raises the necessary cash by borrowing on Ways and Means advances from the Banking Department, creating a balance on 'public deposits' to the credit of the Department concerned. This cash is used to purchase gilt-edged securities from members of the public, who receive in exchange for their securities drafts on the Bank of England which they pay in to the credit of their accounts with the commercial banks. When the drafts are paid (i.e., when the Bank debits 'public deposits' and credits 'bankers' deposits') the result will be a parallel increase in bank deposits and in bank cash, raising cash ratios above the conventional minimum. Subsequently, the bulk of the cash is withdrawn from the banks by a sale to them of tender Treasury bills, the proceeds of this issue being used to pay off the Ways and Means advances extended by the Banking Department. On balance, the public has reduced its holdings of long-term securities and increased its holdings of bank deposits by the same amount; it will be more liquid and interest rates will tend to fall. This increase in the liquidity of the public is the counterpart of a decrease in the liquidity of the Departments, which now hold long-term securities instead of tap bills.

No account of the 'tap and tender' system of finance would

be complete without reference to the operations of one particular and very important Department, namely, the Exchange Equalization Account. This was set up in 1932 to smooth out day-to-day fluctuations in the external value of the pound, but it soon became clear that its operations had important implications for the domestic credit position. At the outset, the Account was endowed by Parliament with borrowing powers of £150 millions, an operation which manifested itself in the public accounts in an equivalent rise of £150 millions in the tap Treasury bill issue.[1] At this point, of course, the operation was a mere paper transaction. Since the assets of the Account were at first all in the form of sterling (i.e. Treasury bills) it could operate only in one direction, namely, to sell sterling on the exchange markets in exchange for gold or its equivalent. However, the influx of capital into this country soon gave the Account the opportunity of acquiring gold.

The resulting operations, as we shall see later, could take place through a variety of channels and stages. For simplicity's sake, however, let us ignore for the present the numerous intermediaries concerned and suppose that an individual Frenchman offers £1,000,000 of gold to the Exchange Account and wishes to receive in return £1,000,000 in the form of deposits with the London commercial banks. The account raises the sterling by turning its tap bills into cash obtained ultimately by a sale of tender bills to the banks, precisely as in the previous example, where we supposed a Department to be switching out of tap bills into gilt-edged. In that example, the Treasury in effect borrowed from the banking system on behalf of the Department to enable the latter to acquire securities; in principle, the methods of financing Exchange Account purchases of gold are identical, and are likely to be similarly reflected in a switch between the tap and tender issues.

Gold continued to flow into this country, as the counterpart of an influx of foreign capital, almost up to the outbreak of war, so that the Exchange Account's holdings of tap bills were

1. This illustrates the point that tap bills, like any other security, need not be issued in respect of actual *cash* handed to the Treasury; compare, for example, the creations of government debt to finance the acquisition of nationalized industries.

steadily depleted. Even before the war its borrowing powers were repeatedly increased by the issue to it of additional bills. The nominal limit set to the borrowing powers was not in practice, however, the limit of its actual borrowing powers, for the Account had at its disposal an additional method of obtaining sterling. It could resell the gold it had acquired to the Issue Department in exchange either for Treasury bills or for notes (the notes themselves, of course, being lodged with the Banking Department and the Exchange Account being credited with an equivalent balance on which to draw).

If the Account had been able to sell gold to the Bank of England at the same price at which the gold had been acquired in the market, then its borrowing powers would in principle have been unlimited; for the initial £150 millions would have been a revolving fund to be turned alternately into gold and then into sterling again as often as required. As it happened, the Bank of England (notwithstanding the depreciation of sterling against gold currencies following the abandonment of the gold standard) could before 1939 buy gold only at the old statutory price of around 85s. per ounce, far below the average market price in those years, which we may suppose to have been 140s. If the Account acquired £140 millions of gold, therefore, it could obtain only £85 millions of sterling by reselling that gold to the Bank of England. If, in turn, this £85 millions was invested in gold, then on reselling this the Account would receive only 85/140ths of £85 millions, and so on. In other words, the effective limit to the borrowing powers, assuming a market price for gold of 140s. and a nominal borrowing limit of £500 millions, would be £1,400 millions.

CHAPTER VIII

THE LIQUIDITY OF BANKING ASSETS

THE general picture we have gained of the discount market and its functions makes it possible to examine with greater understanding the practices of the clearing banks with regard to the disposition of their chief assets. While the assets structure was never completely rigid, the pre-war distribution (which has been largely re-established since 1958) tended within fairly narrow limits to conform to the following pattern:

			As % of deposits
Cash			10
Call money, say	6	'Money market assets'	20
Discounts, say	14		
		'Liquid assets'	30
Investments, say	20–25	'Earning assets'	70
Advances, say	45–50		
			100

To be sure of meeting the demands of their depositors the banks not only maintained a cash reserve of at least 10 per cent of deposits producing no income at all; they also buttressed this actual cash holding with money market assets of about double its own size,[1] the return on which throughout the cheap

1. From the published figures, it is clear that the banks collectively seldom allowed the 'liquidity ratio' (cash, call money and discounts to a percentage of gross deposits) to fall below 30 per cent for any period. To avoid falling below the critical level at the season of peak revenue inflow, higher ratios are maintained at other periods of the year which vary somewhat from bank to bank in accordance with the nature of their business.

money period was extremely small (for long periods only about ½ per cent). For the sake of earnings, however, the banks would be unwilling to see the combined total of these three 'liquid assets' rise much above 20 per cent of deposits, which means that they sought to hold the remaining 70 per cent of their principal assets in the more remunerative form of investment and advances, the two main 'earning assets'. That the bulk of the banks' asset earnings is in fact contributed by these two assets, especially in periods of low Bank Rate, will be apparent from Diagram 6, where the shaded area represents asset earnings on the assumptions – probably not too unrealistic during

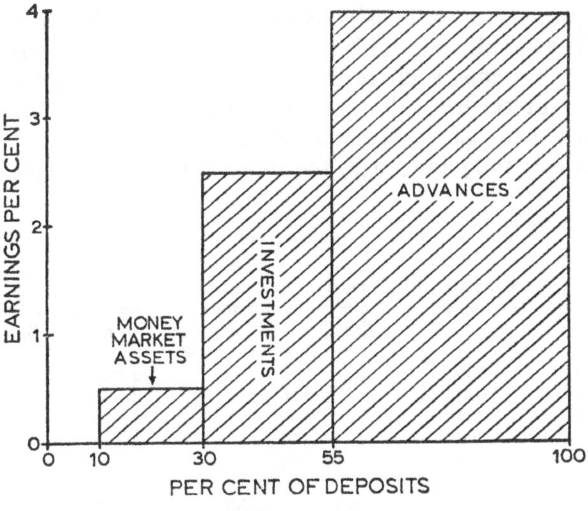

Diagram 6

the later 'thirties – that advances (taken as 45 per cent of deposits) earn 4 per cent, investments 2½ per cent, and the money market assets ½ per cent. (In recent years, of course, yields on money market assets have been much higher.)

It is usually regarded as sufficient explanation to say that this conventional assets structure was determined by the competing pulls of 'liquidity' on the one hand and 'earnings' on the other. The explanation is not, however, a wholly satisfying one; for if the object of holding liquid assets is to be able to meet the claims of depositors, then one would expect the banks, in determining the exact proportion of their total assets to be held in liquid form, to have some regard to the 'quality' of the deposits, i.e., to the likelihood that the depositors will in fact wish to draw out their balances in the form of cash. In particular, if balances are transferred from current account to deposit account the owner of the funds is formally renouncing the right to withdraw them on demand and without notice. Hence one might expect the banks to hold a smaller cash reserve against £100 of liabilities in the form of deposit accounts than against £100 of current accounts, and to allow the overall cash ratio to decline if the proportion of deposit accounts included in the total deposit liabilities should rise. This is in fact the practice in some other banking systems, such as the Federal Reserve System, where the law prescribes a lower minimum cash ratio against time deposits than against demand deposits.

Between 1929 and 1938, the highest annual average for the

TABLE II

Annual averages	*Current accounts* £m	*Deposit accounts* £m	*Other accounts* £m	*Total deposits* £m	*Current accounts as % of total* %
1929	940	798		1,738	54·1
1934*	953	886		1,880	51·8
1939	1,252	996		2,248	55·7
1944	2,765	1,388		4,153	66·2
1949	3,940	2,034		5,974	66·0
1954	4,078	2,094	323	6,495	62·8
1955	4,054	2,070	330	6,454	62·8
1956	3,932	2,008	348	6,288	62·5
1957	3,905	2,139	389	6,432	60·7
1958	3,769	2,442	425	6,636	56·8
1959	4,064	2,431	441	6,935	58·6
1960	4,207	2,515	513	7,236	58·1
1961	4,157	2,638	600	7,395	56·2
1962	4,186	2,747	678	7,611	55·0
1963	4,486	2,781	704	7,971	56·3

* Figures are for ten banks prior to 1936, when the District Bank entered the clearing.

proportion of current accounts was 55·0 per cent in 1937, and the lowest 49·5 per cent in 1932 when the country was in the depths of a slump and any expansionary influence, however modest, would have been a godsend. Suppose that the accepted banking practice had been to keep a 10 per cent cash ratio if current accounts represented 55 per cent of total deposits, and to vary the cash ratio in proportion to any fluctuation in the percentage of current accounts. A decline in the latter to 50 per cent would then automatically have brought a fall in the cash ratio to around 9 per cent, which in turn would have permitted an expansion of some 11 per cent in the volume of deposits supported by a given cash reserve.

Some flexibility of this kind might at times exert quite a useful stabilizing influence. It is true, though only too often forgotten, that responsibility for the monetary situation rests not upon the commercial banks but upon the Bank of England in conjunction with the Treasury, and that with rigid bank ratios the authorities could achieve precisely the desired result by increasing or decreasing the banks' liquid assets. But the vigilance of the authorities has not been so unfailing that any automatic mechanism of the kind suggested should be dismissed out of hand. During the cheap money period, admittedly, the rate of interest that could be earned on a deposit account became so trifling that the banks' customers no longer had any great incentive to keep their current account balances at a minimum and transfer any surplus to deposit account. The distinction between current and deposit accounts thus became blurred but in recent years has regained something of its former importance with the restoration of flexibility to Bank Rate.

So much by way of criticism. Before we pass on to examine the implications of the liquidity conventions, let us pause to consider what we mean by the concept of liquidity as applied to banking assets. In general, one would say that an asset is completely liquid if its owner can count with absolute certainty on turning it into cash (a) at very short notice, and (b) without loss. Applying this concept to bank assets, we discover a fundamental distinction between an asset whose sale or liquidation will merely enable a bank to attract cash from another member of the system, and a truly liquid asset which can be converted into additional cash for the system as a whole. This is most strikingly illustrated by the item 'balances with other banks and cheques in course of collection', which we have not hitherto discussed.

Let us suppose that our system consists of only two banks, each having £100 millions of deposits, and working to a 10 per cent cash ratio, so that each has £10 millions of cash and £90 millions of other assets (call money, discounts, investments and advances); and let us make the further and even more unreal assumption that on a particular day no customer of either bank has drawn any cheques. The balance sheets of the two banks will thus appear as in position (1) of Diagram 7, the combined deposits being £200 millions. Now let us suppose that on the next day the customers of bank A receive cheques for £5 millions drawn by customers of bank B, and pay these into their own bank for collection. We will suppose also that bank A credits either its customers or a suspense account with the equivalent of the cheques they have paid in, before these are presented to bank B for payment. The balance sheet situation will now appear as in position (2) of the diagram: the apparent deposit liabilities of bank A will have increased to £105 millions, the additional deposits having their counterpart on the assets side in £5 millions of 'cheques in course of collection'.

What happens when the cheques are paid? Bank A has to receive £5 millions of cash from bank B, and on the following day this cash will replace the 'cheques in course' item in the former's balance sheet, increasing its cash reserve to £15 millions, but leaving its deposits unchanged at £105 millions. Bank B, on the other hand, loses £5 millions of cash. But what happens to the rest of its balance sheet depends on whether the cheques were drawn by customers possessing credit balances or were drawn against overdraft facilities granted by the bank. In the former case, bank B simply debits its customers for the equivalent of the cheques paid, reducing its deposits by the equivalent of the cash lost, to give the situation shown in position (3) of the diagram. As in position (1), the combined deposits of the two banks again total £200 millions, but bank A holds three-quarters of the combined cash instead of one-half.

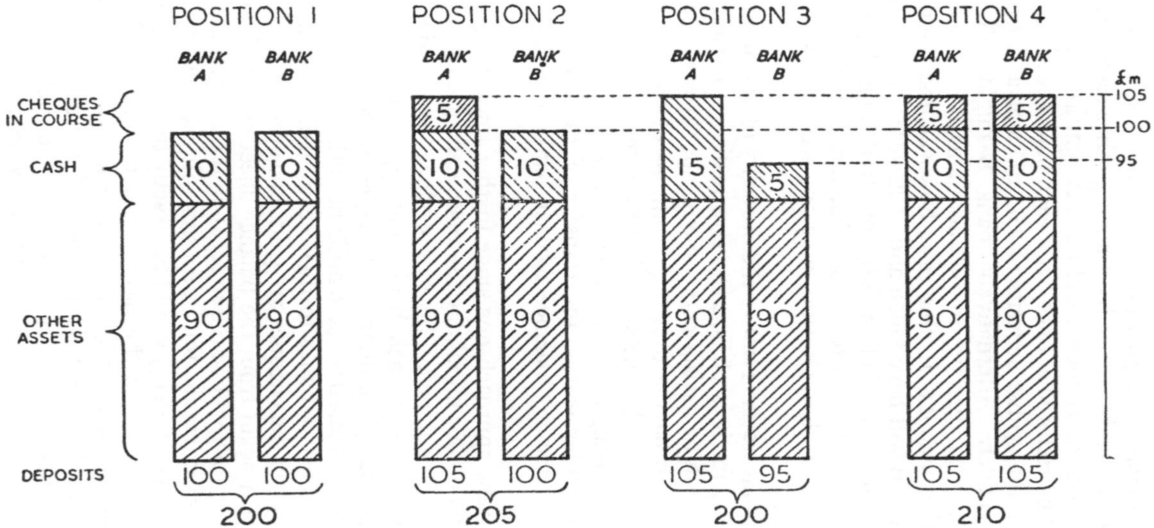
POSITION 1
POSITION 2
POSITION 3
POSITION 4
BANK A
BANK B
CHEQUES IN COURSE
CASH
OTHER ASSETS
DEPOSITS
£m
105
100
95
5
10
15
90
200
205
210

Diagram 7

This is obviously a highly unstable position. Bank B will have to reinforce its cash reserve by realizing other assets. If it sells £4½ millions of investments and bank A acquires them, equilibrium will be restored at once, with each bank showing a 10 per cent cash ratio against deposits of £95 millions and £100 millions respectively. Alternatively, bank B might call in £4½ millions from the discount market and bank A increase its call loans by that amount. In this case, however, the liquid assets ratio of bank B will have fallen and, if it were near the conventional minimum, sales of investments (reducing deposits still further) may be needed to restore that ratio; similarly bank A (with an abnormally high ratio) may buy securities and expand its deposits.

At this point we can remove the unreality of one of our initial assumptions, for it is obviously more realistic to think of this transfer of cash as having come about, not through the customers of bank B having drawn £5 millions of cheques and the customers of bank A none at all, but from the drawings of bank B customers having *exceeded* those of bank A customers by £5 millions. In other words, the transfer of cash will represent only the adverse net balance against bank B in the cheque clearings.

We can now approach one stage further towards reality and suppose that on our initial day the customers of *each* bank draw cheques for £5 millions. This will produce the situation shown in position (4), with each bank holding, in addition to £10 millions of cash, £5 millions of 'cheques in course', and with total deposits increased to £210 millions (although the combined liabilities of the two banks to their customers totals only £200 millions). When the cheques are paid, however, items in course will disappear again from the balance sheet of both banks and no transfer of cash will be required. If all the cheques are drawn by customers in credit, total deposits will also revert to £200 millions, i.e., position (5) would be exactly the same as position (1). To the extent that the payment of the cheques increases debit balances (overdrafts), on the other hand, deposits will be higher than at the outset. In practice, of course, a fresh batch of cheques is being drawn as one day's batch is cleared, so that the banks' apparent deposit liabilities always exceed their true liabilities to the public on the day in question by the amount of cheques in course of collection.[1,2]

The 'cheques and balances' item fluctuates considerably from time to time, and is abnormally large at the half-yearly balance sheet dates, June 30th, and December 31st, when a great many cheques are drawn and still outstanding. For many purposes it is therefore useful to consider not 'gross' deposits as published in the actual statements, but 'net' deposits (i.e., gross deposits less 'cheques and balances'). As already mentioned, fluctuations in 'net' deposits will normally have their counterpart in a corresponding change in the combined total of the five principal assets.

The moral of this discussion is that an asset which may appear highly liquid from the point of view of an individual bank may not add to the true liquid assets of the system as a whole by a single penny. Even the individual bank should report its 'cheques in course' not as an actual reinforcement of the cash holding so much as a safeguard against a severe *loss* of cash; the greater part if not the whole of this item must be set off against cheques drawn by the bank's own customers which will be presented for payment in the immediate future. But in thus showing that the supposed liquidity of the cheques and balances item is largely spurious, we have also demonstrated by implication why investments and advances cannot be counted among the truly liquid assets, even though the securities be those of the British Government and the advances perfectly sound.

To deal with investments first, marketability is not sufficient in itself to render a banking asset liquid. At best, it means that

1. Unless one were to regard overdraft limits granted but not yet utilized as contingent liabilities; but that is not the practice. An omnibus total of unavailed overdraft limits outstanding could in any case be highly misleading. The likelihood of such facilities in fact being drawn upon varies enormously, and in many cases is extremely remote; on the other hand, many customers who have not made formal arrangements for an overdraft limit possess assets normally accepted as banking collateral.

2. The deposit figures also exceed liabilities to the public by the amount of the banks' internal accounts and of balances held with each other. Deposit totals are also inflated by the collection of cheques drawn in favour of customers of the same bank as the drawer, i.e., inter-branch clearings. Only one of the clearing banks (Lloyds) shows these 'items in transit' as a separate item in its balance sheet, but totals for all banks are now shown in the combined statements.

an individual bank, by selling investments to other banks or to customers of other banks, may hope to attract cash from the remainder of the system. If all the banks were selling investments at once, however, even taking it for granted that the general public were willing to absorb the offerings at a price, none of them would in fact gain cash on any scale; indeed, if they were all selling at exactly the same pace there would be no redistribution of cash at all. The situation would then be precisely the same as if each single bank were selling securities to its *own* customers. The only result would be a shrinkage in the investments item on the assets side of the balance sheet, offset by a corresponding decline in deposits on the liabilities side. By selling securities the banks would have reduced their indebtedness to the public, with an incidental improvement in their cash and liquidity *ratios* due to the contraction in deposits; but they would not, collectively, have gained a penny of additional cash.

Very similar considerations apply, of course, to advances. Previous generations of bankers placed great faith in the concept of a 'self-liquidating' asset, such as an advance for some purpose which should place the customer in cash again within a relatively short period, e.g., a loan for the purchase of raw material to be processed. But this only means that the sale of the finished article will enable the customer to build up within a reasonable period a new balance at least equal to the amount advanced; and the only way in which the customer can in fact liquidate his obligation to the bank is by surrendering this balance in discharge of the loan. In building up this balance the customer may have helped to attract cash to his own bank from the other members of the system, or have prevented a loss of cash. But repayment of the advance, as such, will be reflected merely in a parallel decline in the bank's deposit liabilities, on the one hand, and in advances on the assets side of the balance sheet.

Hence a more rigorous lending policy will do little to improve the cash reserve – as distinct from the liquidity ratio – of any bank if all are following the same policy. Moreover, the diminution in the flow of spending (the destruction of incomes) occasioned by the more rigorous lending policy will in turn tend in normal times to cause either unemployment or a fall in prices, and thereby to destroy the 'self-liquidating' character of what would otherwise have been perfectly sound advances. In sum, the element of truth in the idea that a 'self-liquidating' advance is a liquid banking asset lies in the truism that it is healthier for the cash position to make sound advances than to incur bad debts.

What is true of a 'self-liquidating' advance applies equally, in principle, to a commercial bill, however sound the parties and however genuinely short-term the transaction to which it relates. True liquidity is, however, conferred on commercial bills by the practice which allows the discount market to obtain central bank credit against eligible paper. The banks cannot secure additional cash simply by allowing their own holdings of commercial bills to mature; but they can do so by calling in loans secured against commercial paper and thereby forcing the discount market into the Bank. The result is similar if the banks suspend or curtail purchases of Treasury bills. Normally the market will have to finance its purchases of the Treasury bills allotted to it at the previous tender and if the banks curtail their bill purchases (without a corresponding increase in their call loans[1]) will be able to do so only with the aid of central bank credit. On occasions, however, the market can shift the onus of expanding the credit base to the Government, by forcing the Treasury to borrow from the Bank of England to pay off maturing Treasury bills. If December 31st, for example, falls in the middle of a week and the market tenders only for bills to be issued after the crucial date, then on the earlier days of the week it will have no payments to make for fresh bills which would offset the sums due to the market in respect of the bills maturing in the final days of the year. The repayment of those bills must thus be financed, other things equal, by Ways and Means borrowing.

In short, we have at last discovered the touchstone which renders a banking asset truly liquid. This has nothing to do with marketability or the self-liquidating character of the asset;

1. It was not unusual for the banks to curtail bill purchases but to expand market loans before balance sheet dates, thus safeguarding their own liquidity without causing market stringency.

it lies in the power conferred by the possession of an asset to induce the Bank of England to create additional central bank credit, which constitutes bank cash. Liquidity, in other words, depends on what has been called 'shiftability' to the central bank. And in practice this confines the quality of *automatic* liquidity to (a) *maturing* Government obligations, and (b) assets eligible for rediscount with the central bank and held by the discount market.

To analyse the liquidity of the various assets does not in itself explain the conventional assets structure. Why should the opposing claims of liquidity and earnings be exactly reconciled by the maintenance of the conventional liquidity ratios? Since 1918, there have been only two major contractions in bank deposits: during the severe deflation of the early 'twenties and the great depression of the early 'thirties. On each occasion the shrinkage in deposits as a whole was just under 12 per cent, though individual banks saw their deposits contract by as much as 14 or even 19 per cent. Declines of this magnitude do not, however, take place overnight. In the first instance, they were spread over sixteen and in the second over fourteen months; and on each occasion the shrinkage in deposits found its chief reflection in a contraction in money market assets – as shown by the following table:

	Deposits £	*Cash*	*'Cheques and balances'*	*Call money*	*Bills*	*Investments*	*Advances*
Dec. 1921 ..	1,818	226	48	106	424	320	762
Apr. 1923 ..	1,606	192	48	111	250	327	744
Change ..	−212	−34	—	+5	−174	+7	−18
Dec. 1930 ..	1,839	204	54	141	320	270	913
Feb. 1932 ..	1,622	170	41	107	206	265	886
Change ..	−217	−34	−13	−34	−114	−5	−27

(Figures for nine clearing banks.)

It may be concluded, then, that under modern conditions a liquid assets ratio of 30 per cent – until 1963 the conventional level below which the banks did not like the ratio to fall for any length of time – is sufficient to meet any remotely probable loss of deposits. In October 1963 the Governor of the Bank of England announced that a ratio of 28 per cent had been indicated as a suitable minimum for the time being, adding that the banks were prepared under modern conditions to work to a lower figure from the point of view of banking prudence and that the Bank, for its part, would see no objection to a gradual move towards such a lower figure.

There would be general agreement that lower ratios would in no way prejudice the interests of depositors. What must be remembered, however, is that any reduction in the liquidity ratio correspondingly increases the proportion of non-liquid assets, and by definition these involve some element of risk: of temporary depreciation in the case of investments, of bad debts in the case of advances. Hence the relationship between the volume of investments and advances, on the one hand, and of the banks' capital and reserves, on the other hand, cannot be ignored. Movements in these items, as shown by the published figures, are summarized in the tables overleaf.

(*referring to page 89*)

	Deposits	*Advances*		*Investments*	
			As % of *Deposits*		As % of *Deposits*
	£m	£m	%	£m	%
1913	424	280*	61·7	64	14·1
1921	1,768	815	46·1	309	17·5
1939	2,129	943	44·3	564	26·5
1948	5,632	1,257	22·3	1,379	24·5
1956	5,975	1,797	30·1	1,882	31·5
1958	6,306	1,899	30·1	2,045	32·7
1959	6,640	2,498	37·6	1,747	26·3
1960	6,929	3,097	44·7	1,338	19·3
1961	7,081	3,334	47·1	1,064	15·0
1962	6,907	3,393	49·1	1,133	16·4
1963	7,635	3,856	50·5	1,175	15·4

* Loans and discounts (before 1914 mainly commercial bills).

	Actual	*Paid-up capital and published reserves* as % of:*		
		Deposits	*Advances*	*Advances plus Investments*
	£m	%	%	%
1913	38	9·0	13·6	11·0
1921	116	6·6	14·2	10·3
1939	136	6·4	14·4	9·0
1948	149	2·6	11·8	5·6
1956	179	3·0	10·0	4·9
1958	205	3·3	10·8	5·2
1959	260	3·9	10·4	6·1
1960	273	3·9	8·8	6·2
1961	332	4·7	10·0	7·5
1962	401	5·8	11·8	8·9
1963	422	5·5	10·9	8·4

* Including profit and loss account balances.

(Tables are based on yearly averages for nine clearing banks except in case of capital and reserves, where end-year figures are employed.)

CHAPTER IX

THE PRE-WAR ASSETS STRUCTURE

IN the previous chapter we examined the rationale of the conventional pre-war assets structure; let us now consider its implications. The two liquidity conventions, still using the pre-1939 ratios, are: (a) the rule that the cash ratio should never fall below 10 per cent of deposits, and (b) the less rigid rule that the combined ratio to deposits of the three liquid assets should never fall much below 30 per cent. In the absence of a cheap money policy, the chief implication of these conventions is that the volume of credit is completely under the control of the monetary authorities, not in the least under the control of the public nor, except within very narrow limits and over exceedingly short periods, under that of the commercial banks.

Let us consider first the position of the public. There are only two ways in which any person can dispose of his bank balance: he can draw it out in the form of cash or pay it away by cheque. Suppose that the public are on balance drawing out notes. If the Bank of England chooses to neutralize this efflux of notes and restore bank cash to its original level, then the volume of credit will also return to its original level. In other words, it depends directly on the decision of the central bank whether the action of the public in withdrawing notes is allowed to influence the volume of credit. The converse applies, of course, when the public open fresh deposits by paying in to the banks notes formerly in circulation. In the first instance, such a reflux of currency will strengthen the banks' reserve of till money, but it is customary for this to be retained at little more than the bare minimum deemed necessary to satisfy actual requirements. Any excess will be paid in to the Bank of England, not retained to form the basis of an expansion of deposits beyond the immediate knowledge or control of the Bank (which in any case receives periodical returns of till money).

Changes in the amount of currency held by the public, then, will affect the volume of credit only if the Bank of England allows them to do so. Now let us suppose that the public as a whole, feeling short of liquid funds, seeks to build up its balances by refraining from drawing cheques. The only result will be a diminution in the flow of spending. The existing bank deposits turn over less rapidly than before, without in the aggregate increasing by a penny (though if the incidental result is to bring down prices the real command over goods and services represented by those deposits will be enhanced).

There is, of course, yet a third way in which a member of the public can seek to build up his bank balance, and that is by selling securities or other capital assets. We have explicitly assumed, however, that these sales will not be absorbed by the monetary authorities. If we assume also that the liquidity ratio of the banks is at the conventional minimum, it follows that securities sold by one section of the public can be purchased *only* by other members of the public. There will be a transfer of bank balances from the buyers of securities to the sellers, the volume of bank credit remaining unchanged; and the only direct result of the selling will be a decline in security prices (i.e., a rise in yields) needed to tempt the buyers to part with cash and increase their security holdings. It is only if the securities are bought by the banks, or if the Government buys the securities and borrows from the banks to finance their purchase, that the public can, by selling securities, succeed in increasing its combined bank balances.

The position of the banks themselves is only superficially more complicated. Let it be noted that we are not discussing the threadbare question whether or not the banks can 'create credit'. In principle, it is quite obvious that the acquisition by the banks of any asset, unless offset by an equivalent reduction in other assets, will increase the volume of credit, as we have tacitly implied by taking for granted the power of the banks to 'pyramid' on the basis of an addition to their cash reserves. The point is that this power to expand deposits is exercised within a particular framework of conventions. And the effect of these is that *how much* credit the banks can create is, except in the very short run, completely governed by the action of the authorities in providing the banks with cash reserves and, as we shall see, with money market assets.

For the time being, however, let us ignore the liquidity ratio and concentrate on the cash ratio. This was not in fact quite as rigid and inflexible as we have hitherto, for the sake of simplicity, been assuming. The conventional pre-war figure of 10 per cent was merely a *minimum* below which the banks were most reluctant to allow the published ratio to fall. (In the period between the wars it dipped below the 10 per cent level only once, and that very slightly, in October 1936.) Until December 1946, however, the 'published' ratio was habitually lifted above the true cash ratio by the practice of 'window-dressing'. For purposes of their weekly or monthly returns – as distinct from the half-yearly balance sheet dates on June 30th and December 31st – the banks would make up on different days of the week. The banks making up on a particular day would often call in loans from the discount market (raising the cash item in their balance sheet at the expense of call money), while the discount market – if not thereby forced 'into the Bank' – would pay off the called loans with the proceeds of fresh borrowing from the remaining banks. The same result could be achieved by the choice of maturity dates on bills purchased; the banks would each tend to buy bills maturing on their make-up day and to remain out of the market on that day.

In either event the result would be a transfer of cash from the remainder of the system to the bank or banks making up on a particular day, so that part of the available bank cash would operate as a 'stage army'. For each bank individually, the position shown in the statement was, of course, a perfectly accurate one. To aggregate statements relating to different days, however, and so obtain an inflated total for the combined cash reserves, involved a fallacy of composition of the same kind as might result from aggregating, say, the holdings of a particular Government security by a number of extra-budgetary funds whose returns are drawn up on different dates, or the combined cash holding of a number of trading companies having different financial years.

The practice of window-dressing, which always attracted criticism that may seem disproportionate, was abandoned at the end of 1946, when the banks agreed, on the suggestion of the Bank of England, to make up on a common date each month (the third Wednesday),[1] and to aim at a published ratio, which would also be the true and normal ratio, of 8 per cent instead of the former 10 per cent.

It has already been mentioned that during the 'thirties the *published* ratio dropped below 10 per cent on only one occasion. In the other direction the peak cash ratio was as high as 12 per cent, touched in March and April 1934, and ratios of around 11 per cent were not uncommon. At first sight this might suggest that it rested entirely with the discretion of the clearing banks whether every £100 of cash provided by the Bank of England would support only £833 of deposits (with a 12 per cent ratio and no window-dressing), or well over £1,000 (with a true ratio below 10 per cent but levered up to the conventional minimum by window-dressing). It might appear, in other words, that the central bank had in consequence only a very loose control of the situation. The answer is that if the Bank of England were to increase bank cash reserves with the intention of stimulating an expansion of deposits, and instead the commercial banks merely allowed their cash ratio to rise, then the Bank must simply raise bank cash reserves still further. In the first instance this might reflect itself only in a further rise in the cash ratio; but beyond a certain point the pressure which this process would place on the banks to acquire additional assets, and so enlarge their earning power, would become very strong indeed.

Hence it is only in the short run that a desire on the part of the central bank to expand credit could have been frustrated by the action of the commercial banks in allowing their cash ratios to rise above the conventional minimum. Under the new arrangements, fluctuations in cash ratios have been far smaller than in the past. Any variations about the new 8 per cent level are largely fortuitous, due to unforeseen last-minute displacements of funds.

1. Except in June and December, when figures were until 1959 published only for the last day of the month. Since then mid-June and mid-December figures have also been published.

Basically, the abnormally high cash ratios sometimes seen in the past can have had two explanations. During a depression, or at any other time when the business world is lacking in confidence, they may have meant that the banks were affected by the same distrust of existing price levels, including security values, and the same desire to be more than normally liquid, as the rest of the commercial community. As a result, they would be *reluctant* to acquire the additional assets needed if the available cash reserves were to be fully utilized and the cash ratio be brought down to the normal 10 per cent level. Alternatively, the banks may in principle have been perfectly willing to expand their total assets to the necessary extent, but acceptable additional assets might not be immediately *available*.

At this point, we clearly need to look more closely at the processes by which the banks themselves can expand or contract their balance-sheet totals. On a little examination we find that there is only one major asset that at all times satisfies the test of immediate availability: namely, marketable securities. Since there is always an unsatisfied fringe of borrowers, it may seem at first sight that advances, too, could readily be increased by the simple process of refusing fewer applications. That could only be done, however, by lowering the banks' standards of security and creditworthiness.[1] Nor would it be consistent with sound banking principles to permit a slowing down in the flow of repayments of outstanding advances, with the danger of these becoming partially frozen. If lending standards are to be maintained, any major expansion of advances must thus wait upon an expansion in the flow of applications conforming to those standards – a matter in which the initiative must come from the public rather than the banks.

Fluctuations in advances ought not in any case to be regarded as having any direct influence on the size of the banks' total assets, nor, therefore, on the volume of credit. A 'scissors movement' between advances and investments was a normal feature of pre-war banking practice, changes in advances being offset

1. We are here discussing the normal position where security and creditworthiness are the sole criteria of a sound advance. While advances directives were in force (See Appendix) rejected applications would include some proposals turned down as inconsistent with official requests.

by compensating changes in investments to maintain a fairly steady ratio of around 70 per cent for the two items taken together.

We are left with the money market assets, whose supply, given the predominant position of the Treasury bill, is now largely regulated by Treasury policy. Let us start from a position of equilibrium, with a cash ratio of just about 10 per cent and no surplus of liquid assets, and let us suppose that the Bank of England increases bank cash reserves by £10 millions with the object of inducing an expansion of £100 millions in deposits. From the foregoing, it will be evident that the Bank is unlikely to succeed in this aim unless at the same time the Treasury arranges to increase the available supply of Treasury bills to permit an increase of some £20 millions in the money market assets.

This is a very different conclusion from that we should arrive at if we regarded the cash ratio rule as the sole determinant of deposits. It would be easy for the authorities, if they believed that only the cash ratio mattered, to argue that the best way to 'drive the banks into gilt-edged' would be to increase the supply of cash while *reducing* the supply of Treasury bills, so that the banks' money market assets would decline and this would widen still further the gap to be filled by purchases of securities. In reality, as is implicit in the '30 per cent' rule, the contrary is the case. If the supply of bills is not expanded sufficiently to maintain the liquidity ratio, the banks are likely to make smaller, not larger, purchases of gilt-edged. Certainly, they will not utilize any additional cash to the fullest extent by keeping the cash ratio down to the conventional minimum. If the shortage of bills is acute, they may actually *reduce* their combined holdings of investments and advances. A shortage of bills, in fact, will have a strongly deflationary influence – and conversely.

In the years before 1939 there was a great deal of controversy on this subject. In principle, if a bill famine had all the deflationary consequences imputed to it, we should expect to find at least six indications of these effects:

(1) The 'liquid assets ratio' will stand below 30 per cent.

(2) Investments and advances, taken together, will be declining.

(3) This will be reflected in a contraction in deposits additional to that resulting from the shrinkage in money market assets, so that

(4) The cash ratio will be abnormally high.

(5) The dearth of Treasury bills would be expected to show itself in some evidence of increased competition for the available supply, such as a decline in precentage allotments at the weekly tenders.

(6) Finally, the shrinkage in the liquid assets of the public due to the decline in deposits will be associated, other things equal, with declining security prices and a stiffening of yields.

All this is implied by a real bill famine on the pure logic of the '30 per cent' theory. Yet in spite of the reiterated complaints of a severe scarcity of bills at various periods in the 'thirties it is difficult to find many examples of the situation depicted. Periods of bill famine will be apparent at a glance from the chart on page 98. This shows the five main clearing bank assets arranged in the usual order: reading downwards, cash, call money, discounts, investments and advances. Hence the top line of the chart – AA^1 – closely corresponds to the level of net deposits, while the line BB^1 marks the division between the three liquid assets and the two earning assets. The broken line – CC^1 – is so drawn that 30 per cent of net deposits lie above it and 70 per cent below. Hence, periods of bill famine are those in which CC^1 is running *below* BB^1. The 'mountain range' at the bottom of the chart indicates the excess of cash ratio over 10 per cent. It is thus simple to check by inspection whether a bill famine is associated with (a) an abnormally high cash ratio, (b) a decline in earning assets (which means that the line BB^1 will be sloping downwards from left to right), and (c) a decline in deposits (which means that the line AA^1 will be sloping downwards from left to right).

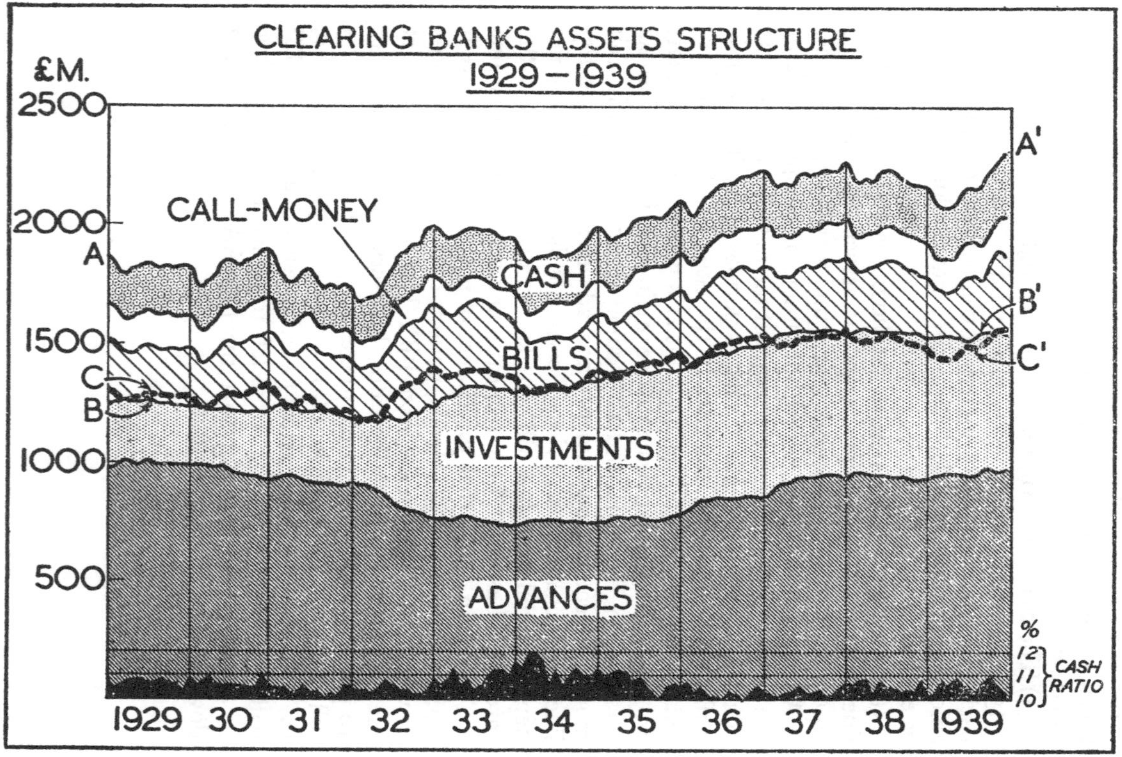
CLEARING BANKS ASSETS STRUCTURE
1929 – 1939
£M.
2500
2000
1500
1000
500
A
C
B
A'
B'
C'
CALL-MONEY
CASH
BILLS
INVESTMENTS
ADVANCES
%
12
11
10
CASH RATIO
1929
30
31
32
33
34
35
36
37
38
1939

Diagram 8

CHAPTER X

THE TECHNIQUE OF INSULATION

IN previous chapters we have seen that the supply of Treasury bills has an important influence on the volume of credit and is involved in the operations of the Exchange Account. It is now proposed to study the technique of Exchange Fund finance in rather greater detail. At first sight such a study may seem, in post-war conditions, of mainly historical interest, but that is not the case. The *modus operandi* of the Exchange Account provides a useful insight into the mechanics of Government borrowing generally, and is therefore relevant to such questions as the technique of cheap money. Moreover, the operations of the Exchange Account serve to illustrate the relationship, under *any* exchange régime, between the external balance of payments and the domestic monetary situation.

The Exchange Equalization Account was set up by the Finance Act of 1932 – nine months after our departure from the gold standard – for the purpose of smoothing out day-to-day fluctuations in the rate of exchange. It was conceived, in other words, as a steadying influence on the exchange market, to be a seller of sterling when that currency was in strong demand, and of gold (which means, of other countries' currencies) if a pressure on sterling threatened to depress its value in the exchange markets. This alone, however, would not distinguish the operations of the Exchange Account from the normal activities of the Bank of England under gold standard conditions; for the obligations imposed on the Bank of England to buy or sell gold without limit at a fixed price[1] meant that the supply of sterling in the exchange markets was automatically adjusted to the demand for it, and with such precision that fluctuations

1. Actually to buy gold at £3 17s. 9d. per standard ounce and sell it at £3 17s. 10½d.

in the exchange rate were confined within the extremely narrow margin of the gold import and gold export points. This almost complete stability in the exchange value of sterling, however, might be achieved only at the cost of considerable fluctuations in the volume and price of domestic credit, for every influx of gold would tend to generate a *multiple* expansion in the volume of credit, and conversely.[1] That is undoubtedly the correct response if the influx or efflux of gold reflects the position of the country's balance of payments on current account (i.e., an export surplus or an import surplus). It may well be the appropriate response, also, if the gold inflow forms the counterpart of an influx of genuine capital, whose physical investment, such as the building of a factory, will result in additional *income* being paid out by the domestic capital goods industries. But this concertina expansion and contraction of credit, with its repercussions on the level of domestic incomes, is certainly not the appropriate response to a movement of short-term capital seeking security, whose owners will hold it in liquid form while it is in the country and may whisk it off at a moment's notice to some other international centre if that should appear to offer greater attractions.

Two features thus distinguish the functions of the Exchange Account from those of a central bank operating under gold standard conditions. First, a central bank buying or selling gold (i.e., selling or buying its own currency), does so with the object of defending a particular external parity for its currency. The Exchange Account was set up, as we have seen, shortly after our abandonment of the gold standard, and this at a time when it was not desired to fix the exchange value of sterling at any particular level, when our policy, in other words, was that of a 'floating pound'. Hence the Exchange Fund was not supposed, in its operations in the exchange markets, to resist any decided trend in the value of the pound one way or the other, but merely to prevent sharp fortuitous fluctuations in the exchange rate from day to day.

One might suppose, from what has been said above, that the

1. The essential stages, in brief, are: the Banking Department buys gold (passed on to the Issue Department in exchange for notes), paying with a draft on itself which the seller of the gold pays in to his bank, whose cash reserve is thereby increased, permitting a pyramiding of assets on the basis of this additional central bank credit.

object of such a policy might be to maintain the pound at its equilibrium level in terms of the balance of payments on current account; that is, to allow the pound to appreciate only in so far as its strength resulted from an export surplus and to depreciate if it came under pressure as the result of over-importing, thus using the rate of exchange as a means of restoring the balance on current account.

In reality, no clear distinction was made in Parliament between pressures due to the balance of payments on current account and those resulting from capital movements. Admittedly, it would be difficult in practice to differentiate at all exactly between these two sets of factors. Yet some people may feel that possible advantages were lost in the failure to make the attempt. If one allowed the pound to appreciate in the exchange market simply because foreign capital was pouring into London, at a time when the sterling area was unable to balance its payments on current account, this must mean still further handicapping our exporters and encouraging imports, thus widening still further the deficit on current account. Similarly, if heavy withdrawals of foreign capital were allowed to depress the value of sterling at a time when the sterling area already had an export surplus on current account, this would accentuate an existing under-valuation of the pound. However, the policy laid down for the Exchange Account was not to seek to maintain the exchange parity for sterling at its equilibrium level by offsetting all short term capital movements, but to remain neutral in face of all sustained pressures, whether on capital or current account.

Secondly, and this brings us back to the internal effects of Exchange Account finance, the Fund was intended to insulate the domestic credit structure against disturbances due to the inflow and outflow of gold. Under gold standard conditions, as we have seen, the purchase or sale of gold by the central bank had its counterpart pound for pound in an increase or decrease in the cash reserves of the commercial banks, whose pyramiding tended to produce an expansion or reduction in bank deposits of many times the amount of the gold movement. It was thus thought at first that the mere purchase and sale of gold by the Exchange Equalization Account, instead of the Bank of England, by depriving the gold movements of any effect on bank cash reserves, would entirely insulate the domestic credit structure against external influence. Yet, paradoxically, in the years before 1939 it was the operations of the Exchange Account that were held responsible for most of the disturbances to credit which in fact occurred.

Let us see how this came about. The Exchange Account was set up in 1932 with initial borrowing powers of £150 millions, provided in the form of an issue of 'tap' Treasury bills. The issue of these bills was, of course, reflected immediately in a corresponding rise in the nominal total of the floating debt, yet at that stage nothing more had happened than a mere book entry, with no effect whatever on the credit structure. Such effects could only arise when the Fund began actual operations; and since at the outset the Fund had little or no foreign exchange assets, these could only take place in one direction: namely, through sales of sterling (obtained by selling the Treasury bills with which the Fund had been endowed) in exchange for gold. Let us now imagine a situation which was, in fact, of pretty common occurrence during the 'thirties, namely a flight of capital from France to Britain. A number of Frenchmen wish to hold £100 millions of sterling bank deposits instead of francs, the Bank of France sells gold to offset the resulting pressure on the franc, and the Exchange Equalization Account finances the purchase of that gold by selling Treasury bills to the commercial banks, whose deposits show an equivalent expansion.

Leaving out some intermediate stages, we then have the following chain of transactions, or, rather, the following manifestations of a single movement of funds between the two countries:

French public:	Receive sterling (in form of credit balances with British banks).	Surrender francs (formerly held on deposit with French banks).
Bank of France:	Reduces its deposit liabilities (out of francs received from French banks in payment for sterling sold to their customers).	Sells gold.
Exchange Account:	Receives gold.	Sells Treasury bills.
British banks:	Receive Treasury bills.	Add to their deposit liabilities (by additional amount held for credit of French customers).

At first sight it would seem that the movement of funds has been completely neutralized. The exchange rate between the two currencies will not have been affected, because the supply of sterling has been increased to meet the demand; the French public now hold, instead of francs, the £100 millions of sterling which they desired; and this has come about through the creation of an additional £100 millions of deposits, leaving the British public with exactly the same volume of deposits as before. Moreover, the influx of gold has not (as it would have done in gold standard conditions) increased the *cash reserves* of the commercial banks by a penny, so that there will be no tendency for any multiple expansion of credit on that account. On the other hand, the liquidity ratios of the banks will have risen, while in the first instance their cash ratio, as a result of the rise in deposits, will have fallen.

To see how far insulation has been achieved, in other words, we need to look far more closely at the effects of Exchange Account operations on banking ratios and the assets structure of the banks. The problems will emerge most clearly if, once again, we consider a simplified arithmetical example, using purely hypothetical figures.

Position of Commercial Banks

	I	II	III
	£m	£m	£m
Cash	120	120	110
Money market assets ..	150	250	250
Other assets	730	730	740
Deposits	1,000	1,100	1,100

At the outset we may suppose the situation of the commercial banks to be that shown in Position I. The first point to note is that the cash ratio is as high as 12 per cent, or well above the pre-war conventional minimum. Clearly, there has to be some slack in the cash ratio, for without that the transaction could not take place in the form assumed above. Instead of allowing their deposits to rise, the banks, if their cash ratio were already at the bedrock level, could take up the Exchange Account's sales of Treasury bills only by reducing their other assets: that is, the combined total of investments and advances. The domestic public would have either to buy securities sold by the banks or pay off part of their indebtedness to the banks. In either case, the domestic public as a whole would be called on to surrender £100 millions of deposits (in effect transferred to French customers, leaving the deposits total unchanged). This reduction of the domestic public's liquid assets would have a strong deflationary tendency and many of the refinements of Exchange Account technique have to be devised to counter this.

That the cash ratio at the outset is above the normal minimum is, then, a necessary assumption. A glance at the figures is sufficient to show why this situation exists: the banks are suffering from a serious dearth of bills and the liquid assets ratio is well below the desired minimum of 30 per cent. Position II shows the situation after the influx of gold has been financed. The bill famine has been more than rectified, for discounts and call loans are now equivalent to more than 22½ per cent of deposits. Moreover, the cash ratio still stands at nearly 11 per cent even of the increased volume of deposits, giving a liquid assets ratio of over 33½ per cent.

In principle, this is not an equilibrium position. Fortified by their now abundant secondary reserves the banks are likely, other things equal, to allow their cash ratios to fall back towards a more normal level; which means that they are likely to add to their investment portfolios and expand their deposits in the process. This secondary expansion could be prevented only by open-market operations on the part of the Bank of England designed to mop up any surplus cash. Let us suppose that the authorities in fact sell £10 millions of securities to the banks, reducing their cash reserves to £110 millions (Position III).

With the cash ratio down to the conventional minimum and the liquid assets ratio only moderately above the 30 per cent minimum, the position may be assumed to be a stable one. What happens now if the Exchange Account has to finance a further influx of gold? In the first place, it is obvious, since there is no slack in the cash ratio, that this cannot be financed wholly by the sale of Treasury bills to the banks without causing a deflationary pressure, as described above. To avoid that, it must be so financed that the banks receive at least the minimum of additional cash required to support any additional deposits.

To leave the cash ratio unaffected, the Fund must so conduct its operations that, of every £100 millions of finance it requires, only £90 millions is obtained from the commercial banks and the remaining £10 millions from the central bank.[1] Even this does not necessarily mean, however, that complete insulation will have been achieved, for each part of these operations may still have secondary repercussions.

Let us first consider the effect on the Bank of England. There are two methods by which the Exchange Account can obtain finance from the central bank: by selling to the Bank of England *either* Treasury bills or gold. If it sells Treasury bills, the result is to increase on the one hand the deposit liabilities of the Banking Department and on the other hand that Department's holding of Government securities; the expansion in the assets and liabilities of the Department will be accompanied by a fall in the Proportion (since the Reserve of coin and notes will be unchanged). A sale of gold by the Exchange Account to the Bank has precisely the opposite result. In effect, the Exchange Account receives for the gold additional notes which it pays in to the Banking Department for the credit of its account, so that in this case the expansion in the deposit liabilities of the Banking Department has its counterpart in an addition to the Reserve, with a resulting rise in the Proportion. As has been said, it is of the essence of central banking that the Proportion – in contrast with the cash ratio of the commercial banks – should be allowed to fluctuate within reasonable limits. Before 1939, however, when the Proportion was still of some interest to overseas observers if not our own people, it would probably have been considered undesirable to allow the figure to fall very low, as would occur if the Exchange Account were to retain the whole of a large influx of gold and sell only Treasury bills to the Bank. Through a suitable combination of gold sales and Treasury bill sales, however, its operations can be prevented from affecting the Proportion at all. If it were desired, for example, to stabilize the Proportion at 30 per cent, then of every £10 millions of finance required by the Account from the Bank

1. Given the present-day 8 per cent ratio, of course, 92 per cent of Exchange Account finance must be obtained from the commercial banks and only 8 per cent from the central bank.

of England, £7 millions should be obtained by sales of Treasury bills and £3 millions by sales of gold.[1]

What of the commercial banks? We have seen that a 10 per cent cash ratio would be unaffected provided the Exchange Account obtained from the Bank of England £10 millions out of every £100 millions of finance required. This does not, however, change the fact that the counterpart of the remaining £90 millions of additional deposits will be provided entirely by money market assets. An expansion in deposits due to Exchange Account finance will thus tend to be accompanied by a rise in the 'liquid assets ratio'.

Let us return to Position III as shown on p. 103 and suppose that the Fund has to finance a further influx of £100 millions, which it does in the manner we have been assuming, to produce

Position of Commercial Banks

	III £m	% of deposits	IV £m	% of deposits
Cash	110	*10·0*	120	*10·0*
Money market assets	250	*22·7*	340	*28·3*
Other assets	740	*67·3*	740	*61·7*
Deposits	1,100	*100·0*	1,200	*100·0*

Position IV. The cash ratio is unchanged at 10 per cent; but money market assets are now equivalent to more than 28 per cent of deposits, so that the ratio of earning assets is below 62 per cent, instead of the pre-war norm of 70 per cent. Obviously, there will be a strong tendency for the banks to expand their earning assets. On the one hand, they will reinforce the cash reserve by realizing money market assets (forcing the market 'into the Bank' by calling in loans, or allowing bills to run off). This will tend to create stringent conditions in Lombard Street, reflected in rising money and bill rates. On the other hand, the banks will be buyers of securities, so that the price of short-dated gilt-edged will tend to rise and yields to decline correspondingly.

If we think of the Treasury bill rate as typifying the short-term rate of interest, and the yield on gilt-edged securities as

1. See pages 76–7 on effect of difference between market price of gold and statutory price.

typifying the long-term rate, then we can say that an indefinite increase in money market assets will begin to place an upward pressure on the short-term rate and a downward pressure on the long-term rate.

This can be neutralized if the authorities themselves sell short-dated bonds and use the proceeds of these sales to retire Treasury bills, so that in the balance sheets of the banks investments take the place of money market assets. This gives us a further refinement in the methods of finance demanded by a policy of complete insulation. In reality, it is merely one more implication of the general principle underlying the whole chain of argument, which can be stated thus: *To achieve complete insulation, the Account must so conduct its operations as to leave undisturbed (a) the volume of liquid assets available to the domestic public, and (b) the conventional banking ratios.*

Hitherto we have been dealing only with the simplest case in which the overseas buyer of sterling is assumed to wish to hold his claim in the form of a bank deposit. In the first instance, indeed, overseas claims to sterling will universally be created in that form. Application of our general principles clearly indicates what is demanded by a policy of insulation if the foreigner wishes ultimately to acquire sterling in various other forms. Let us suppose, for example, that he wishes to acquire and hoard bank notes. For the Exchange Account this means that the *whole* of any gold influx which forms the counterpart of note hoarding must ultimately be financed by an equivalent increase in the note issue; for any other policy will deplete first the till money of the commercial banks and secondly – as the latter replenish their till money by drawing on their balances at the Bank of England – the Reserve of the Banking Department.

In the first instance we may suppose the influx to have been financed in the manner least likely to cause disturbance if the foreign funds were to remain with the commercial banks: namely, by the sale to the latter of £90 millions of Treasury bills and to the Bank of England of, say, £7 millions of Treasury bills and £3 millions of gold. As the foreigners draw out their deposits in the form of notes, however, the cash reserves of the banks will be depleted, and that can only be prevented if, in effect, the Bank of England buys back, in exchange for the notes it supplies, the Treasury bills originally sold to the commercial banks. But this process will deplete the Reserve of the Banking Department and reduce the Proportion unless the Banking Department can in turn exchange these Treasury bills for additional notes. Indeed, if the whole of the foreign balances are switched from deposits into notes, the Bank must also be able to exchange for notes the assets originally acquired direct from the Fund. That can be done either by selling the Treasury bills to the Issue Department as the counterpart of an increase in the fiduciary issue, or to the Exchange Account in exchange for gold which is passed on to the Issue Department as the backing for additional notes.

In practice, it is far from easy to gauge whether a particular drain of notes is due to foreign or domestic demands, and before the war more than one severe stringency was allowed to occur before the correct technique was understood and applied. In principle, however, note hoarding presents no obstacle to complete insulation, for the basic reason that the supply of notes, like the supply of bank deposits, is within the control of the authorities, and can be increased to any extent needed to satisfy an external demand. Without going into the details of further examples, we can, in fact, lay down the further generalization that *complete insulation is possible in all cases, but only in those cases, where the supply of the type of asset in which the foreigner wishes to hold his sterling claim can be varied by the authorities at will.* This means that the only additional cases in which complete insulation is theoretically possible are where the foreigner wishes to hold Government securities, whether marketable gilt-edged or short-term securities such as Treasury bills.[1] Such demands are basically a demand for government credit, just as a demand for notes is a demand for central bank credit and a demand for bank deposits is a demand for commercial bank credit.

The case is different if the foreigner buys sterling with the object of acquiring any asset whose supply is not susceptible to variations in this way on the initiative of the Exchange

1. If the foreigner wishes to acquire gold, we can regard this analytically as a reversal of the original gold inflow, even if the gold were to be held in safe deposit in this country.

Account. In practice, a great deal of French money found its way during the 'thirties into gold shares or copper mining shares purchased in London. This means that some bank deposits created on behalf of French buyers of sterling were transferred to the domestic public in exchange for such mining securities. Hence the former holders of the securities would find their liquid funds increased, and in turn could bid up the price of other securities on the domestic Stock Exchange. By extinguishing all or part of the additional credit the Bank of England can, of course, prevent foreign buying of mining shares from generating a general boom on the Stock Exchange. But the initial transfer of some particular securities into foreign ownership means that the final position could not be absolutely identical with the first; *perfect* insulation is not even theoretically attainable.

The practical possibilities of achieving complete insulation are further restricted not only by the difficulties of exact diagnosis (which are, of course, formidable), but by the inevitable time-lag involved in some of the necessary adjustments. Thus, before the war it was not common practice for the commercial banks to have large direct dealings with the Bank of England. Hence the conversion into notes of large amounts of Treasury bills held by the banks, to meet a sudden wave of foreign note hoarding, could normally be achieved only by the process of 'driving the discount market into the Bank' with much incidental disturbance to short-term interest rates.[1] The necessary contraction in the tender Treasury bill issue might be attainable only by reducing the amount offered for several weeks in succession; and in the meantime the assumed note hoarding would be subjecting the cash reserves of the banks and the Reserves of the Banking Department to serious strain. Similarly, a sudden withdrawal of funds would mean a sharp inflow of funds to the Exchange Account in payment for its sales of foreign exchange. In the first instance, this involves a transfer from the balances of the commercial banks at the Bank of England to the Funds' account with that institution (i.e., a transfer from bankers'

1. To a certain extent this was prevented by the operations of the 'special buyer', but the authorities were slow to adapt their technique to the exigencies of Exchange Account finance.

deposits to public deposits), and some time might elapse before the funds could be returned to the banking system.

In short, we can say that, while the institution of an Exchange Account affords a high degree of protection to the domestic credit structure against external disturbances, the possibilities of insulation, even in theory, are not unlimited, and in practice inevitably fall far short of perfection. During 1936, for example, the cash reserves of the banks were subjected to serious strain by a sustained foreign hoarding demand for British notes that was only countered after considerable delay by vigorous purchases of gold on the part of the Bank of England. In the following year, again, Lord Keynes (basing his argument on Mr. F. W. Paish's figures), showed that the Fund had been exerting a deflationary pressure for a different reason. From January to September 1937, he estimated that the Exchange Account had acquired some £190 millions of gold; yet over that period both the volume of bank credit and the oustanding amount of tender Treasury bills actually declined. In effect, Lord Keynes argued, the influx of gold had been financed, not by the banking system, but largely with money drawn out of the pockets of the domestic public, the chief items being £104 millions from the proceeds of a Defence Loan and other long-term issues, £60 millions from the current surplus of the Unemployment Fund and other extra-budgetary funds, and £12 millions from current Government revenue. By using this money to finance an influx of gold, Lord Keynes said, 'the managers of the Exchange Account largely depleted the liquid resources of the domestic market'.

At the time it was widely felt that Lord Keynes should have directed his criticisms at the Treasury's policy as a whole rather than its management of the Exchange Account in particular: the important thing was that, through the Funding Loan and in other ways, deposits had been taken away from the domestic public, not that the deposits had been placed at the disposal of foreign holders of sterling. The most serious complaint against the Exchange Account, it was suggested, was that its operations enabled the other, deflationary, transactions to be hidden from the public gaze. What is undeniable is that the funding of Treasury bills clearly reduced the liquid assets of the domestic public below the desired level, as indicated by the fall of over 10 points in the price of Consols during these nine months. On the other hand, this deflationary pressure caused no apparent disturbance to the economy as a whole; industrial production was rising and unemployment fell by more than 300,000 during the period in question.

At the beginning of this chapter it was said that the operations of the Exchange Account illustrate, among other things, the relationship under any exchange régime between the external balance of payments and the domestic monetary situation. The connection can be most clearly visualized if we suppose the gold movements to reflect the position on current account. Imports, let us say, exceed exports. The payments which British importers have to effect in foreign currency exceed the amounts of foreign currency which British exporters are currently earning and selling on the exchange market. If sterling is not to depreciate, importers will have to cover the balance of their requirements for foreign currency with exchange acquired by the Exchange Account as the proceeds of sales of gold abroad. (In practice, the operations in gold and foreign exchange will, of course, be handled by the Bank of England and other banking intermediaries.) The Exchange Account will be receiving sterling from British importers in payment for its sales of foreign exchange; and that sterling, like the net receipts of any other extra-budgetary fund, will automatically be lent to the Exchequer and so become available to finance either the current expenditure of the Government or the repayment of internal debt. In other words, we have the seemingly paradoxical situation that an adverse balance of payments is a source of revenue to the Exchequer.

Let us suppose that, with the country's external payments exactly in balance, the Government faces a budget deficit of £100 millions: it must either impose an additional £100 millions of taxation or create £100 millions of internal debt by borrowing from the public or the banking system. What is the position if, instead of the balance of payments being in equilibrium, there is an external deficit of £100 millions? Even if the budget is left in deficit to the extent of £100 millions there will be no need to borrow from the banks; the budget deficit will in effect be financed by the sale of gold. Similarly, if the budget were exactly balanced, the proceeds of the gold sales would permit the redemption of £100 millions of effective debt, in exactly the same way as a budget surplus.

It is not for a moment suggested that it is sound practice to finance a budget deficit by using up the country's external reserve. The point is that the *effect* of an import surplus on the Exchequer position and the domestic credit situation is identical with that of an equivalent increase in taxation. Both are in principle deflationary.[1] And the deflationary effect of the import surplus is unaffected by the precise methods by which it is financed. If it is financed by an overseas loan, for example, the Exchange Account will accumulate sterling through the sale of the resulting foreign exchange proceeds in precisely the same way as if it were selling gold.

The monetary effects are unchanged where the import surplus consists of a free gift of goods from abroad, and therefore does not have to be financed at all. This was essentially the situation under Marshall Aid. In effect, such overseas grants place the Government in possession of goods bought - with free dollars - overseas; the goods are then sold on the domestic market and the sterling proceeds accrue to the Exchequer. If the budget (in the wider sense which includes capital as well as revenue transactions) is balanced, this sterling can be used only to redeem internal debt; it did so, in fact, quite automatically and independently of the elaborate accounting methods (the hocus-pocus of 'special accounts' held by the Bank of England) devised by the Economic Recovery Act to ensure that it was in fact used for that purpose.

The Government does not accumulate cash, except over very short periods, but must return cash to the banking system through debt repayments in order to avert severe deflationary pressures. It is therefore a truism that any excess of receipts from all sources (including the proceeds of overseas loans or gifts and the realization of external assets) over total expendi-

1. Not simply from the financial point of view. An important surplus brings goods on to the home market which have been produced abroad and whose production has not generated any domestic income. Conversely, with an export surplus, the goods leave the country but the incomes generated in their production remain behind.

ture will necessarily extinguish an equivalent amount of internal debt. Nothing is really gained by 'earmarking' particular receipts for that purpose. It is only if the earmarking compels a government to spend less than it otherwise would have done (which may have been the case in some other countries) that the special account procedure can achieve any useful purpose.

All these repercussions of the external balance of payments on the domestic credit situation represent particular examples of a more general proposition. When the Exchange Account is selling gold or foreign exchange, the Government sector is liquidating a capital asset and receiving payment from the domestic public and/or the banking system. When the tide is running the other way the Government sector is acquiring a capital asset; and that asset must be paid for either (a) out of a current surplus of Government receipts that would otherwise have been available to redeem internal debt, or (b) with the proceeds of new borrowing from the public and/or the banking system. This remains true, whatever the nature of the capital asset sold or acquired. It applies, for example, if Government trading departments are increasing or liquidating their stocks of goods. More important, from the monetary point of view, it applies if Government departments are increasing or reducing their holdings of securities, a case that will occupy our attention when we come to examine in detail the mechanism of cheap money.

CHAPTER XI

THE NOTE ISSUE SINCE 1939

AT first sight, and to some extent even in principle, the Currency and Bank Notes Act of 1939 was a revolutionary departure in the management of our finances. Under the Bank Charter Act of 1844 additional notes could be issued only against additional gold, valued at a fixed statutory price of about 85s. an ounce, which remained unchanged for nearly a century. The 1928 Act, as we have seen, envisaged increases in the fiduciary issue, but only with the explicit authority of Parliament if an increase temporarily sanctioned by the Treasury had not been reversed within two years, and so promised to become a permanent addition to the note issue. The automatic safeguard against inflation provided by the gold link having been abandoned in 1931, the remaining safeguard of Parliamentary approval seems on the face of it to have been thrown overboard by the 1939 Act, which introduced an entirely new principle for the regulation of the note issue. It provided that the size of the note issue should always be equal to the *market value* of the gold and other assets held by the Issue Department. In other words, the note issue could be expanded if, without any change in the physical holding of the Issue Department, there was a rise in the market price of gold; and since a rise in the market price reflects a depreciation of sterling, not only against gold but against any other currency linked to gold, this logically turns the basic principle of the gold standard and the 1844 Act upside down.

What helps to place the 1939 Act in proper perspective is the fact that even before the war the fiduciary issue had come to make up the bulk of the note issue. The Act retained the procedure of Parliamentary sanction after two years for any increase in the fiduciary issue above a basic level (raised from the £260 millions of the 1928 Act to £300 millions). If Parliament were in fact apprehensive of inflationary results from an expansion of the note issue due to a rise in the market price of gold it need only refuse to sanction the maintenance of a fiduciary issue in excess of £300 millions or, of course, order the issue to be reduced – though the consequences of either course might be devastating.[1] The true revolution in our finances, in short, came with the abandonment of the gold standard in its full rigour and the statutory recognition of the will of Parliament, instead of the automatic index of the balance of payments, as the arbiter of the appropriate size of the money stock. It was this change-over to a managed currency that was fundamental. Once that all-important step had been taken, for better or worse, further changes, however revolutionary in appearance, could affect only the technique of management.

Let us now examine the 1939 procedure in detail. The Act provides (Section 2) for a weekly valuation of the assets of the Issue Department, and (Section 3) for settlement between the Bank and the Exchange Account of any differences thus revealed between the size of the outstanding note issue and the market value of the assets held as backing, laying down further that:

> 'Any payment required by this sub-section may be effected in cash or, by agreement between the Treasury and the Bank of England, by a transfer of gold or securities (whichever is appropriate), or partly in cash and partly by such a transfer.'

It will be seen that three methods of payment are prescribed: transfers in cash, in gold and in securities. The effects of each method can best be illustrated by taking hypothetical figures. We will suppose that at the outset the total note issue is £500 millions, of which the fiduciary issue represents £400 millions, the remaining £100 millions being backed by gold valued at 85s. an ounce, and that the price of gold is then exactly doubled. The value of the assets in the Issue Department is now £600 millions, and £100 millions is owing to the Exchange Account. To take the simpler case first, if the difference is settled by a gold transfer, all that happens is that one-half of the Issue Department's gold holding is paid over to the Exchange Fund.

1. See pages 120–3.

The note issue remains at £500 millions, the fiduciary issue at £400 millions, and the gold holding at £100 millions; in the Bank Return, the only sign of what has happened will be a change from 85s. to 170s. per ounce in the price at which that gold is valued.

If, on the other hand, the difference is settled in cash, the note issue rises to £600 millions, of which £200 millions is backed by gold, valued at 170s. The additional £100 millions of notes in theory belong to the Exchange Account, which we may suppose to pay them in for the credit of its account with the Banking Department. On the assets side of the Return, the Reserve goes up by £100 millions, as the counterpart of an increase in public deposits on the liabilities side. Provided nothing more happens, however, the actual credit base (i.e., the level of bankers' deposits) is not affected; and it is in fact improbable that the additional money should find its way into bankers' deposits, since the Exchange Account is not likely to be selling sterling to acquire gold at a time when sterling is already depreciating against gold. That being so, it is equally unlikely that the Fund should wish to hold its £100 millions in the form of idle cash. The obvious course would be for the Fund to use this cash to buy securities, normally Treasury bills, from the Banking Department. If that is done the net effect of the operation is simply to increase the Reserve while reducing the securities holding by the same amount, thus raising the Proportion but leaving the total assets and liabilities of the Banking Department unchanged. Similarly, settlement in cash of a difference due to a fall in the price of gold will in all probability merely reduce the Proportion while leaving the credit base unaffected.

What are affected by the choice between cash transfers and gold transfers, then, are (a) the Reserve of the Banking Department rather than its total assets and liabilities, and (b) the distribution of the Exchange Account's assets as between gold and sterling. In the case of differences arising out of changes in the value of the Issue Department's securities, the same general principles apply, except that cash settlement of a difference due to an appreciation in securities will normally be impossible without special authorization of a fresh increase in the fiduciary issue, since (at £300 millions or over) this will normally be standing at the maximum level permitted under existing authorizations.

To illustrate the working of these principles, it will be useful to study some examples of their application in practice. The following table shows the Bank Return changes associated with the initial revaluation of gold at market prices:

Date 1939	Notes Issued £	Fiduciary Issue £	Gold £	Valued at: (fine ounce) s. d.
February 22 ..	526,414,357	400,000,000	126,414,357	84 11.454*
March 1	526,414,475	300,000,000	226,414,475	148 5
March 8	526,033,091	300,000,000	226,033,091	148 2
March 15	526,033,091	300,000,000	226,033,091	148 5

* Equivalent to former statutory price of £3 17s. 10½d. per ounce, *eleven-twelfths* fine.

On the gold held by the Issue Department on February 22nd, 1939, the revaluation 'profit' was about £94½ millions. Had this gold simply been revalued and the fiduciary issue reduced by £100 millions, the total issue would thus have fallen by about £5½ millions. On March 1st, however, the Bank announced a gold purchase of £5,567,000, so that the total issue was in fact left virtually unchanged (it rose by £118). The price of 148s. 5d. was the price 'fixed' in the bullion market on March 1st, and included a premium of 1½d. over the dollar parity on that day (i.e., over the sterling equivalent, at the current exchange rate, of the United States buying price for gold of $35 an ounce).

The price of 148s. 2d. taken in the March 8th Return was ½d. below the fixed price of the day, doubtless to emphasize that the Bank enjoys some latitude in certifying a price to be the current one 'on the day of valuation, ascertained in such manner as may be agreed between the Treasury and the Bank'. It will be seen that the gold holding and therefore the total issue show a contraction on the week of £381,384. This is exactly equal to the depreciation by 3d. an ounce of the physical gold holding indicated by the previous return. In other words, the difference arising from the fall in the market value of that gold was settled in cash, i.e., by the surrender and cancellation of £381,384 of notes, to the debit of the Exchange Account. In the following week the certified price or gold is up by 3d., but no change is shown in either the gold holding or the total issue. It follows that the difference had been settled by a transfer of (51,593·6 ounces of) gold to the Exchange Account.

On the outbreak of war, the price of gold (reflecting a depreciation in the exchange value of sterling) rose sharply: from 148s. 6d. in the August 23rd Return to 168s. in that of September 6th. The Issue Department's gold holding was first written up proportionately, raising the total issue from £546·4 millions to £580·1 millions, and then all but the odd £102,189 was transferred to the Exchange Account. Thereafter, changes in the market price of gold could obviously have only quite negligible effects on the size of the note issue. This may be illustrated by the Bank Return movements associated with the devaluation of September 1949:

Date 1949		Notes Issued £	Fiduciary Issue £m	Gold £	Valued at: (fine ounce) s.	d.
September 14	..	1,350,247,833	1,350·0	247,833*	172	3†
21	..	1,350,356,823	1,350·0	356,823	248	0‡
28	..	1,300,356,823	1,300·0	356,823	248	0

* Small transfers of gold had been made to the Issue Department in 1939 and 1940, and the gold price of 168s. adopted in 1939 (which was appreciably below the theoretical dollar parity at $4.03) was raised to 172s. 3d. on June 13th, 1945, as an adjustment to the decline in insurance rates and other costs with the ending of war-time shipping hazards.

† Theoretical parity with the dollar 173s. 8½d. at $4·03, and 250s. at $2·80.

‡ The increase of £108,990 in the gold reserve and the total issue shown by the September 21st Return corresponds exactly to the rise in the gold price, i.e., the difference in favour of the Exchange account was settled in cash. In the following week, it will be seen, the fiduciary issue was reduced by £50 millions – not a remarkable movement with the Reserve around £90 millions, though its timing (given the imminence of the Christmas drain) may suggest a desire to reassure home and overseas observers nervous about possible inflationary implications of the devaluation.

Fundamentally, then, the 1939 Act was nothing more than a change, and in responsible hands an improvement, in the technique of operating a managed currency. So far as monetary principles are concerned, it serves merely to emphasize the rather farcical nature of 'backing' for an inconvertible currency. The Issue Department has been endowed with 'assets' whose market value must henceforth exactly equal the outstanding total of the notes which form its 'liabilities'. Accountants may in consequence feel happier. But the only real liability of the Issue Department under present conditions is to supply nice, clean pieces of paper in exchange for old notes.[1] The plain man may therefore well enquire in what way the Department is better equipped to discharge that function through the possession of other pieces of paper called securities.

The principle involved is really applicable not only to the Issue Department, but to all Government 'Funds'. It turns on the question whether any really useful purpose is in fact served by the practice of Government departments and extra-budgetary funds in holding as their 'assets' parcels of governmental promises to pay at various future dates. The case of the Unemployment Fund (now merged in the National Insurance Fund), will serve as illustration. If over a period unemployment insurance levies exceed by £100 million the allowances paid, £100 millions of debt formerly held by the public passes in effect into the possession of the Fund. Yet the possession of those particular securities does not in any true sense represent a 'fund' of resources that will better enable the Fund to effect payment of unemployment allowances if at some future period its current receipts should prove insufficient to cover its current disbursements. Should that happen, the money it requires will have to be raised afresh through the use of the Government's general borrowing powers. It is this access to general Government credit that constitutes the real security that unemployment allowances will be paid. The so-called accumulated 'assets' of the Fund are no more than a record that in the past the Fund's income has exceeded its disbursements by that amount (less, of course, accumulated interest and any subsequent appreciation in the particular securities given to it at the time, or plus the amount of any depreciation).

The alternative method of accounting would be to cancel any Government debt which finds its way into the hands of the public sector. Any accumulation of Departmental or extra-budgetary receipts, or any increase in the volume of currency,

1. Either a new note or, if notes are returning from circulation and the limit is reduced, interest-bearing securities in exchange for notes surrendered by the Banking Department.

would then reflect themselves in a decline in the national debt. To adopt this system, however, would raise the almost insoluble problem of deciding where the private sector ends and the public sector begins.

To return to the question of the note issue, the persistent inflation of incomes and prices since 1939 has, of course, brought an enormous increase in the demand for currency. The succession of increases in the fiduciary issue made under Defence Regulations raised the total issue to an average of £1,311 millions in 1945, or about two and a half times the 1939 average of £548 millions. During this period, therefore, the expansion in the currency circulation was running well ahead of that in money incomes, which rose by little more than half.

In the early post-war years it was thus possible to bring down the fiduciary issue on balance from the end–1946 peak of £1,450 millions to £1,300 millions in the first half of 1950. Thereafter, the currency circulation began rising again in step with the continued growth of money incomes. In the abortive bill of 1952 (crowded out by other Parliamentary business) the basic level of the fiduciary issue was fixed at £1,400 millions. This was raised to £1,575 millions for the 1954 Act but was exceeded a few weeks after the Act came into force and has been continuously exceeded ever since, the fiduciary issue reaching £2,475 millions at the Christmas holiday peak of 1960.

From 1952 to 1955 the growth of the currency circulation closely paralleled that of money incomes, as measured by the gross domestic product; since then the currency circulation has lagged behind the growth of incomes, as will be seen from the following table:

	Gross domestic product	*Currency circulation*		*Gross domestic product*	*Currency circulation*
1952	100	100	1958	145	139
1953	107	107	1959	152	144
1954	114	113	1960	162	151
1955	121	121	1961	173	157
1956	132	129	1962	180	158
1957	139	134	1963	189	162

The rising tide of currency has led some observers, who rightly hold that inflation is a monetary phenomenon, to suggest that the problem of holding down the money supply should be tackled by placing a fixed limit on the fiduciary issue. The reasoning behind this view is that the Bank of England would then no longer be able to neutralize a drain of currency into circulation by transferring securities from the Banking Department to the Issue Department in exchange for additional notes. It would be forced to return to the techniques of the classical gold standard: namely, to allow the drain to reduce bank cash, thus creating stringent conditions in the money market, and seek to defend the Reserve by raising Bank Rate to any level that might be needed to fight off the demands upon it. Under gold standard conditions this process was usually successful, though it was necessary on more than one occasion to suspend the Bank Act and authorize an issue in excess of the legal limit.

This approach is inconsistent with the now generally accepted view that it is regulation of the total liquid assets of the banks, not an attempt to regulate the proportion of those assets held in the form of actual cash, that provides the key to control of the monetary situation as a whole. A little consideration of the relevant magnitudes will show that to adhere to a fixed limit to the fiduciary issue while an internal currency drain was still in progress would, if persisted in, cause a complete breakdown of the national finances. In practice, therefore, an increase in the issue would have to be sanctioned retrospectively (by the equivalent of suspending the Bank Act) instead of concurrently, as at present.

In 1962, notes and coin outstanding averaged £2,717 millions, of which £2,161 millions was in the hands of the public and £555 millions held by banks, as follows:

	£m
Bank of England Reserve	47
Clearing Banks (till money)	365
Scottish and Irish Banks*	143

* As backing for their own notes of roughly equivalent amount in circulation.

Source: Statistical Digest.

Bankers' deposits at the Bank of England average £246 millions and the total deposit liabilities of the Banking Department £502[1]

1. Including £172 millions of Special Deposits.

millions. The liquid assets of the clearing banks averaged £2,546 millions, to give a liquidity ratio of 33·5 per cent against deposits of £7,611 millions.

In 1963, the estimated circulation with the public averaged £2,220 millions, an increase of £59 millions on the year. Let us suppose that in 1962 a fixed limit had been placed on the fiduciary issue and that the figures quoted above for the clearing banks (in fact averages for the whole year) represented their position when this was done. The drain of currency into circulation – reflecting an antecedent rise in incomes – continues.

If the clearing banks met the first £47 millions of the drain by drawing on their balances with the Bank of England (which they regard as equivalent to actual cash), the Reserve in the Banking Department would be exhausted within a few months. The Bank would then have no means of meeting its remaining liabilities on bankers' deposits of £199 millions (nor, of course, its other deposit liabilities). The Bank, in other words, would have to suspend payment.

Meanwhile, the cash and deposits of the clearing banks would each have fallen by £47 millions. Assuming that the cash ratio at the outset was at its minimum they would need to reinforce the cash reserve by some £43 millions to restore the normal ratio. To do this they would in normal circumstances only have to realize money market assets, the liquidity ratio still being over 30 per cent. If they sought to raise the additional cash by calling in money, the discount market would be forced on to the Bank's doorstep but would have to be turned away again. Similarly, the Treasury would have to be refused if the banks allowed their Treasury bill holdings to run down and the Treasury was unable to meet its maturing obligations by raising money from the public.

Such a situation, obviously, could never be allowed to occur. In the meantime, of course, Bank Rate would have been forced up to crisis levels; but the potential demands on the Reserve being so large, no rise in Bank Rate, however drastic, could serve to protect a Reserve of less than £50 millions under the conditions assumed.

It is only if the liquidity ratio at the outset were at its minimum that the loss of cash would necessitate sales of investments and bring downward pressure to bear upon the level of deposits. Even then, however, the operative factor would not be the loss of cash as such but the reduction in total liquid assets below the minimum needed to support the existing volume of deposits. If we ignore the effect of a rise in Bank Rate upon the demand for advances (which may or may not be significant) precisely the same result could have been achieved without dislocation by a funding of Treasury bills.

Since the object of the exercise is not to precipitate a financial crisis but to bring pressure to bear upon the level of bank deposits, the moral is clear: that it is more sensible to operate directly upon bank deposits by tempting money out of the banks into long-term securities. Under modern conditions, in other words, the key to control of the money supply is a proper funding policy.

CHAPTER XII

BANK RATE AND ITS WORKINGS

In previous chapters we have seen that under modern conditions a change in Bank Rate,[1] by itself, cannot be expected to exert the same technical effects upon the money supply as in former times. Nevertheless, the psychological effects of a change, both upon the domestic public and the outside world, remain important – and influencing the expectations of the business world is an integral part of monetary management. Hence Bank Rate can still provide a useful weapon in a crisis, as recent events have demonstrated. Unless it is assumed that future policies will be successful in preventing crises from occurring, therefore, the controversies about the *modus operandi* of Bank Rate cannot be deemed of merely academic interest.

Historically, the Bank Rate technique evolved as part of the mechanism of the gold standard. The amazing promptitude with which a rise in Bank Rate usually succeeded in stemming a gold outflow was undoubtedly due mainly to the effect of a rise in short-term rates, relatively to those in other financial centres, in curtailing London's foreign lending and attracting balances from abroad. Money in London having become dearer than elsewhere, London acceptance credits would be repaid and replaced by borrowings in other centres. At the same time, the enhanced yield obtainable on sterling bills would stimulate the famous Continental investment demand for them. For both purposes, funds would have to be remitted to London.

The efficiency of this mechanism depended largely on that unquestioned confidence in the stability of exchange rates which was the essence of true gold standard conditions. If owners of foreign balances feel that there is any risk of a de-

1. For Bank Rate changes since 1930 see table on page 139.

preciation of the currency in which they are investing, they will tend to 'hedge' their position (i.e., make a forward sale of the currency equal to their spot purchase of it), and this will tend to produce a forward discount on the currency which subtracts from the interest yield obtainable on the investment. For example, if three months' sterling bills yield 6 per cent, but the exchange market quotes sterling for delivery three months forward at 1 per cent discount, the return to a (covered) foreign buyer of sterling bills will not be 6 per cent, but only 2 per cent per annum. Hence, if the balances initially attracted by a rise in Bank Rate are hedged, and this increases the forward discount (or reduces the forward premium) on the currency, even extremely high Bank Rates will fail to attract funds on any scale. On the contrary, very high interest rates will be needed to prevent an outflow of funds (in the form of a constantly renewed bear position) from a country whose forward exchange stands at an appreciable discount.[1]

Such difficulties will be only temporary if the maintenance of high interest rates re-establishes confidence in the existing exchange rate, reflecting itself in an improvement in the forward quotation. Even so, if the volume of short-term balances liable to move from one international centre to another is very large in relation to central bank gold reserves, a centre in which short-term interest rates lag behind those prevailing elsewhere will be threatened by serious losses of gold. It will therefore be very important for the various central banks to keep their rates more or less in line with each other, so that a rise in Bank Rate in any one country will tend to be followed with great promptitude by other members of the system. This goes far towards accounting for the highly volatile fluctuations in Bank Rate which were typical of gold standard conditions. (See chart on page 141.)

In the first instance, then, the main effect of a rise in Bank Rate under gold standard conditions was to induce a liquidation of London's short-term assets and an increase in London's short-term liabilities, obviating the need for continued gold shipments. But a shift in international short-term lending is clearly no more than a temporary expedient, filling a gap in

1. On all this, see P. Einzig, *Theory of Forward Exchange*.

the balance of payments for an interval, but doing nothing to remove the causes of the initial disequilibrium. The Bank Rate mechanism could never have operated so efficiently unless it exerted at the same time some influence on internal activity, high rates tending to depress employment and (in nineteenth-century conditions) also money wages and prices, thereby tending to discourage imports and encourage exports.[1]

Whether any such influence is sufficiently explained by a change in short-term rates as such, or derives from changes in the long-term rate induced by Bank Rate changes, has been the subject of much theoretical controversy, as has the precise nature of the connection between the two rates. Fortunately, it is not incumbent for our purposes to plunge at all deeply into these problems, but a brief outline of the issues involved is necessary to any examination of the monetary mechanism.

Most discussion starts from the proposition that if, at the current level of interest rates, borrowers can see more than normal expectations of profit they will expand their activities, and conversely. There would clearly be no difficulties if it could be taken for granted, as was formerly done, that the additional interest burden due to a rise in short-term rates within the normal range of fluctuation will itself suffice to make all the difference between expectations of abnormally high and merely normal profits, or between expectations of normal profits and fears of loss. Unfortunately for that straightforward solution, the interest burden imposed on borrowers by a rise in short-term rates appears a very small item of cost in relation to the profit margins which entrepreneurs normally expect before embarking on an operation at all. That is the basic difficulty which has to be faced in any attempt to derive the effectiveness of interest-rate changes from their influence on costs and therefore on profit margins. It is largely resolved, of course, if one believes that there is a class of marginal projects which will be just worth while at any given level of interest rates, but will be abandoned as unprofitable in the face of even a relatively small

1. It is now recognized that the emergence of an import surplus, which tends to reduce the national income, will thereby tend also to reduce the demand for imports: but this will merely prevent the disequilibrium from becoming cumulative, not restore equilibrium.

increase in costs resulting from higher interest rates. Instances of this kind can no doubt be found, especially where the factor of high 'gearing' is present.[1] Nevertheless, so many other elements in cost can exert so much greater an influence on expected profit margins that the primacy accorded in economic theory to changes in interest rates (and which experience seems on the whole to justify) is difficult to substantiate by this line of argument.

One of the leading authorities, Sir Ralph Hawtrey, argues that interest charges are in fact a very significant element in the cost of carrying stocks of goods against borrowed money, so that a rise in short-term rates will be quite sufficient to cause merchants to draw in their horns. The reduction in their stocks will mean a falling off in the flow of replacement orders, depressing manufacturing output and slowing down the pace of economic activity in general. In Sir Ralph Hawtrey's view, in other words, the direct effect of the rise in short-term rates is alone sufficient to account for the observed facts, leaving nothing to explain. Rightly or wrongly, this diagnosis is no longer widely accepted as satisfactory in itself. In particular, the late Lord Keynes, while agreeing that Sir Ralph Hawtrey's analysis is on the right lines, argued that it errs in concentrating exclusively on one type of investment, namely, investment in working capital, 'to which a degree of sensitiveness to changes in Bank Rate is attributed which certainly does not exist in fact'.

The really important effects of Bank Rate, on the Keynesian view, derive from its influence on the long-term rate of interest.

1. To take a hypothetical example in order to illustrate the principle involved, let us suppose that a factory which cost £5½ millions to build can be let at an annual rental of £220,000, equivalent to 4 per cent on the cost of construction. If the undertakers of the enterprise can float £5 millions of debentures at 3 per cent, they will make an annual return of £70,000, equivalent to 14 per cent on their own investment of £500,000, of which 11 per cent can be regarded as the reward of risk-bearing, managerial ability, etc. If the debenture rate rises to 4 per cent, the entrepreneurs will themselves obtain a return of only 4 per cent, or no more than they could earn by investing their own funds in debentures, and the enterprise will clearly not be worth while. The effect on profit margins of a rise in interest rates will be multiplied by the amount of the 'gearing' (in this case, borrowed capital equal to ten times the equity investment). In principle, of course, all this applies equally to merchants trading on borrowed capital and thus assists Sir Ralph Hawtrey's diagnosis.

Higher Bank Rates, it is argued, will be associated with higher bond rates,[1] thus depressing the value of existing capital instruments, including long-term securities, and of new fixed capital. In general terms, this means that the value of all durable goods will decline without – in the first instance – any change in the cost of producing them. Hence there will be a decline in the output of the capital goods industries, 'for there is no sense in building up a new enterprise at a cost greater than that at which a similar existing enterprise can be purchased'. We shall thus see a fall in employment and (given any degree of flexibility) in money wages and prices, including export prices. In any case, the foreign balance will be improved by a reduction in imports, due to the fall in employment and incomes; if wages and prices also decline, part of the improvement in the foreign balance will come from an increase in exports. Conversely, in a depression, low Bank Rates may in the first instance stimulate recovery by increasing the price level of existing investments, the price of new capital goods rising in sympathy.

Before examining the implications of this line of thought we have to enquire whether movements in Bank Rate will in fact induce sympathetic changes in long-term rates, for even that is open to dispute. At first sight, some of the statistical evidence

1. In the same way that Bank Rate symbolizes the whole complex of short-term rates, so bond rate is sometimes used to symbolize the whole complex of long-term rates, i.e., in addition to the yield on Consols the rate used to capitalize durable physical assets (houses, factories, plant and equipment), as well as the yield on claims to such assets, i.e., on industrial securities of all classes, including equity shares. As we shall see, however, such a use of the expression is highly misleading: for while a rise in the yield on Consols always implies a fall in their price, a rise in the yield on industrial equities may accompany a *rise* in their price if dividends are increasing still more rapidly. There is the further difficulty that the only basis on which industrial yields can be computed is by reference to dividends actually paid in the past. Let us suppose that during an inflationary boom Consols are yielding 5 per cent, that an industrial share which received a 4 per cent dividend in the previous year is standing at par on the expectation that the dividend will be doubled, but that in the event the dividend is left unchanged. The yield on industrials will then appear to have dipped below the yield on Consols, but this does not change the fact that even during a boom investors *expect* a higher yield on industrials than on government securities, precisely because it is realized that dividend expectations are liable to be falsified in this way. The consequences attributed to a rise in bond rates will in fact occur only if gilt-edged and industrials are declining side by side, i.e., after a boom has broken.

may seem to negative the idea of any connection at all between Bank Rate and Consols. To take a typical period under gold standard conditions, when the interest rate technique was operating on the whole with fair success. we find that during the thirty-four years from 1845 to 1878 the margin between the highest and lowest Bank Rate in any one year averaged about $2\frac{3}{4}$ per cent. Yet the five years in which Consols showed exceptionally small movements of 3 points or less were years in which Bank Rate moved on the average by nearly $3\frac{1}{2}$ per cent, while in the eight years in which Consols fluctuated by 8 points or more the average variation in Bank Rate was only $2\frac{1}{8}$ per cent. Over the whole period, in which Bank Rate twice rose as high as 10 per cent and several times dipped as low as 2 per cent, the highest and lowest prices for Consols were 102 and $78\frac{3}{4}$, giving a yield of just under 3 per cent and just over $3\frac{3}{4}$ per cent respectively. After 1855 the fluctuations in Consols were limited to 14 points, from $98\frac{3}{4}$ to $84\frac{5}{8}$.

When one examines the figures in greater detail, the relationship begins to seem more impressive, if not at first sight wholly convincing. In the period from September 1844 to October 1878 we find as many as 81 'turning points' in the movement of Bank Rate, with an average range of 2·4 per cent. So large a number of movements, incidentally, with an average duration of only four and a half months for the upswings and downswings, may suggest that the changes can have had little relation to the characteristic trade cycle lasting several years, and indeed we know that Bank Rate was fixed primarily, if not exclusively, with reference to fluctuations in the gold reserve, not the level of internal activity. But many of these upward and downward movements were of a very minor nature. The crisis peaks, with Bank Rate reaching levels of 7 per cent or more, were spaced at more decent intervals separated by some years; and most of the really large rises and falls in Consols were in fact associated, as one would expect, with these major upswings in Bank Rate to crisis levels and the subsequent return to very cheap money. That is not, of course, to say that it was the rise in Bank Rate which *caused* the fall in Consols; both may have been affected by common influences, such as boom and slump, financial crisis or fear of war.

Taking the 81 upward and downward movements as a whole, we find that on 55 of these occasions a rise in Bank Rate was associated with a decline in Consols, and conversely. The remaining 26 instances, in which Consols moved in the contrary direction, represented small movements averaging only three-quarters of a point, and were normally associated with relatively small swings in Bank Rate (averaging 2 per cent; in twelve instances 1½ per cent or less). In some cases these contrary movements may suggest that the Stock Exchange may have shown somewhat greater prescience than the monetary authorities. The fact remains that in a substantial proportion of cases Consols actually rose side by side with Bank Rate and frequently showed remarkably little reaction to quite drastic movements in Bank Rate. By present-day standards, the stability of Consols, in the face of these spectacular fluctuations in conditions in the short-term market, was remarkable.

The statistical evidence, then, as to the relationship between Bank Rate and Consols requires rather careful interpretation. But a pretty clear picture emerges of Bank Rate as highly volatile and fluctuating widely and at short intervals, above and below a long-term rate which by contrast is extremely stable but so far as it moves at all normally varies in the same direction as Bank Rate. What light have general considerations to throw on the question? Sir Ralph Hawtrey, who is so emphatic that a rise in short-term interest charges represents a decisive factor in the cost of carrying stocks of goods, argues that they can have little effect on the price of long-term securities. He points out, for example (*A Century of Bank Rate*), that if Bank Rate rises from 3 to 7 per cent, but is expected to revert to 3 per cent in three months' times, 'the extra cost of holding a long-dated security with borrowed money would be offset by a fall of price equal to 1 per cent (the equivalent of 4 per cent per annum for a quarter of a year). A trader who had intended to raise a bank advance to cover some expenditure might be led by a rise of the interest on the advance from 3 to 7 per cent to sell government securities instead. But if the price of the government securities fell from 100 to 99, he would not gain by doing so.'

While the arithmetic is impeccable the choice, as Professor

Hawtrey recognizes, is not one that is likely to confront any trader in practice. This balancing of a loss of interest and capital value, through the sale of a long-term security, against a short-term interest charge, depends on the explicit assumption that the restoration of Bank Rate to 3 per cent exactly three months ahead can be foreseen with certainty. But it tacitly assumes also that the trader can foresee with equal certainty that the price of the long-term security three months ahead will be exactly 100. Any such assumption is, of course, completely unrealistic.

In practice, the trader's reasoning must surely be that it will pay him to sell the securities, at any price, in order to finance his operation if he feels reasonably confident that he can buy them back again three months hence at a price not more than 1 per cent higher than the current level, however the latter may compare with that ruling before the increase in Bank Rate. It is not apparent why the Bank Rate movement should induce either a fall of exactly 1 per cent in the Consols price or the confident expectation of a recovery by 1 per cent within three months. If the trader expects the price of gilt-edged actually to decline (or to rise by less than 1 per cent over the three months) it will, of course, pay him to sell regardless of past changes in price.

Fortunately, we do not have to rely upon such calculations to show that sympathetic connections do in fact exist between short-term and long-term rates. They cannot fail to do so, since short-term borrowing and the liquidation of long-term securities are often alternative means of raising cash, while investors often have the alternative of short-term or long-term lending. Hence, there are any number of ways in which conditions in the market for short-term credit and the values of long-term capital assets may act and react on each other, due especially to the important institutional connection between the two markets through the Stock Exchange, the money market and the commercial banks. If industrial securities are declining the times will not be propitious for the flotation of new capital issues; intending borrowers from the capital market will seek increased bank accommodation until prospects improve, and if the banks themselves are fully expanded the resulting increase in advances will require them to sell investments and so put pressure on the long-term rate. Again, gilt-edged jobbers as well as the discount market customarily finance part of their portfolios by means of bank credit: if the charge for such accommodation should rise they will tend to lighten their books.[1]

More generally, in a boom situation characterized by high Bank Rates and expanding credit, advances will tend to rise more rapidly than the banks' liquid assets, so that bank selling of investments may be superimposed on realizations by entrepreneurs. Conversely, advances usually fall off in the later stages of a depression, permitting the banks to expand their securities portfolio.

Given these inter-connections between the markets for short-term and long-term capital, what has to be explained is why the long-term rate normally remains so extremely stable notwithstanding the (normally very drastic) movements in short-term rates. On the face of it, this is a poser for any theory which seeks to explain the influence of Bank Rate by its influence on the long-term rate. Part of the attraction of the transfer of attention to the long-term rate lies in the fact that it is in the case of extremely long-term investments – notably building – that interest charges are an important element in costs, and it is a matter of common observation that the level of activity in building, with the numerous ancillary industries dependent on it, has an especially important influence on the level of trade in general. Yet if the long-term rate is so highly stable – normally we must think in terms of changes of a fraction of 1 per cent – its variations may be no more significant in relation to the normal profit expected from an investment in durable goods than are the much larger changes in the short-term rate relatively to the expected profitability of investments in working capital.

Again, part of the attraction of looking to the long-term rate as the main regulator of activity lies in the changes in the capital value of existing securities which form the obverse of any change in the long-term rate, and which seem likely to exert a strong

1 It is not necessary that the rate for bank credit should actually exceed the yield on the bonds; a mere narrowing of the margin between the two may make it no longer worth while to accept the risk of a fall in the market value of the bond.

influence on the timing of economic decisions. A rise in the long-term rate from 3 to $3\frac{1}{8}$ per cent corresponds to a fall in the price of an irredeemable 3 per cent stock from par to 96, the equivalent of sixteen months' gross interest on the stock (or well over two years' net return to a holder liable to tax at 7s. 9d. in the pound). Should prices fall by even a small amount, therefore, a holder will be no better off than if he had sacrificed any interest return on his money and postponed his purchase for a considerable period; if a slight downward movement in prices creates any feeling of uncertainty about the future trend of values one would expect an abrupt withdrawal of buying support. This implies, however, that gilt-edged prices will be highly volatile, whereas they are usually remarkably stable.

This may be explained by appealing to the concept of a 'norm' of prices. At any particular time, it is suggested, the investing community will have, consciously or otherwise, a pretty definite feeling about what it expects the *average* level of security prices to be for some time ahead. Market prices will then have difficulty in diverging at all widely from this norm; for a moderate fall will make speculators in the gilt-edged market feel pretty confident that prices are 'too low' and their supporting purchases will check the fall, and conversely. So long as nothing happens to undermine the idea of the norm, therefore, fluctuations will be confined within a relatively narrow range. This does not conflict so flatly as may seem with the previous suggestion that the slightest uncertainty about the future trend of prices will cause a sharp postponement of buying, and conversely. For few operators can feel so supremely confident of their judgment that they would commit themselves to a single price as their forecast of the future level of values; the concept of the norm means that prices are expected to fluctuate within a given range. It is only movements between these upper and lower limits that may have a sharply unsettling effect on the market; once prices move near to either of the extremes, stabilizing purchases or sales will occur.

In thus explaining the stability of the long-term rate, however, we have seriously undermined any case for the efficiency of the Bank Rate mechanism based upon sympathetic movements (whether induced by changes in Bank Rate or merely coinciding with them) in the long-term rate. For it implies that, once gilt-edged prices have fallen to the 'support level', a further rise in Bank Rate will thereafter be quite impotent to lever up the long-term rate any further. If, therefore, Bank Rate operates primarily by affecting the long-term rate, changes beyond a certain point will become quite ineffective. And that is, indeed, what seems to happen. So long as business confidence is high, entrepreneurs will be ready to sell gilt-edged to finance an expansion in their activities, while private investors will be ready to sell gilt-edged in order to subscribe to new issues to industrial capital; but if such sales are easily absorbed (thanks to the speculative support for the gilt-edged market which we have postulated), there will be no dramatic fall in gilt-edged prices to deter either active entrepreneurs or subscribers to industrial shares.

The resulting stability in the yield on gilt-edged is often held to be a most disrupting factor, tending to feed a boom and perpetuate a depression. During a boom, it is argued, when it is desirable to restrain the flow of spending, holders of gilt-edged will sacrifice relatively little either in the form of income or on capital account if they sell securities in order to acquire industrial securities or physical assets. Efforts to create a general stringency of credit by raising interest rates will be countered by the flow into active industrial use of formerly idle balances, tempted into investment in gilt-edged by a quite modest fall in their price. But there is another side to this question. In such a situation the authorities can issue new long-term securities on a large scale without dislocating the gilt-edged market and apply the proceeds of such issues to reduction of the floating debt and of bank deposits. The implication of this line of thought, as of so many others, is the importance of an enlightened and vigilant funding policy.

To speak in terms of boom and slump, however, is tacitly to admit that no theory of the *modus operandi* of Bank Rate can set out to claim that the Bank Rate technique, at least as operated in the past, will serve to keep the economy at all times on an even keel. What we need are obviously two separate theories, (1) to explain why even very high interest rates may for a time be quite powerless to restrain a boom, or very low ones to end depression, (2) to explain how high interest rates may *eventually* bring the boom to an end. At first sight there may seem no reason why a boom should not feed on itself for ever; for, once it has begun, the rise in prices and incomes will tend still further to enhance the expected profitability of enterprise, and to an extent that can easily outweigh any rise in interest rates within the normal range of fluctuation. Why should this process ever be reversed? In principle, one can detect several reasons why a boom may break:

(1) The first has no connection with interest rates. It is the fact that in an open economy a boom will bring an expansion in imports relatively to exports, which will have a restraining influence on prices and tend to falsify the more buoyant expectations of profit. If the upward movement is confined to the country concerned, this factor alone may be sufficient to check the rise in activity at an early stage; it will manifest itself to a much smaller extent if the boom is world-wide, i.e., if incomes and prices are also rising throughout the rest of the system.

(2) The second and in practice probably the decisive factor is a check to the increase in the supply of money. Indeed, it simplifies the whole problem to think of high interest rates as an automatic reflection of a tight monetary situation rather than as a causal factor. During its early stages, the expansion in activity will be financed by a rise in the rate of turnover of bank deposits[1] and, if there is any slack in banking ratios, by an increase in the volume of deposits. But the rise in incomes will eventually lead to an absorption of currency into circulation (and also, in a monetary régime of gold standard type, to conversion of notes into gold for export in settlement of an adverse foreign balance). Even if the central bank were to leave Bank Rate unchanged, therefore, an internal drain will bring about some reduction in the liquid assets of the banks.

(3) It may be objected that Bank Rate even at peak levels (and, indeed, especially by the time the boom has gone far enough for Bank Rate to have reached peak levels), may fall far short of expected profit margins. The answer is that there are times when credit may be not merely dear but, for large

1. For example, through sales of gilt-edged on the part of industry, which thus secures command of formerly idle balances.

classes of traders, in practice unobtainable. Even in normal times the allocation of credit, especially through banking channels, is not decided merely by the rate of interest; a trader cannot be sure of obtaining credit on any scale he desires simply by offering to pay a higher rate.

In their customers' interests as well as their own, the banks simply do not operate on that principle. If they feel that an advance involves an unjustifiable risk they will not be tempted to make it by the offer of an abnormally high rate, and if they feel that the operation is justified the advance will be made at the normal rate. Hence at any time there is usually an unsatisfied fringe of borrowers (or of borrowers who would like more accommodation than their banks feel justified in allowing). At a time of real stringency the fringe will become a very wide one indeed; and it will include, incidentally, some of those operators whose supporting purchases of gilt-edged are in more normal times responsible for the stability of the Consols rate. In short, recorded interest rates apply only to the transactions which actually take place and may not measure the equilibrium price of credit. At a certain stage large numbers of entrepreneurs will find it impossible to finance the completion of additions to fixed capital or the carrying of inflated stocks of finished and semi-finished goods. Once this happens prices will collapse, possibly to the accompaniment of a wave of bankruptcies, and the bubble will burst.

(4) Before this crisis stage has been reached, the boom may conceivably bring itself to an end through a collapse in the level of business confidence. Just as we have supposed the investing community to have a definite feeling about the norm of gilt-edged values, so traders may have a definite feeling about the norm of prices in general. At a certain stage the more prudent among them will begin to feel that prices are becoming 'too high'; they will reduce their demand for finished goods and for the factors of production, exerting a restraining influence on the level of activity as a whole. Secondly, experience may have taught a sufficient number of traders to interpret a rise in Bank Rate as a warning of possibly far more stringent conditions to come, with the ultimate threat of bankruptcy for any trader who finds himself over-expanded at a time of crisis.

If the business community in fact react in this way, and begin to haul in sail in response to quite small advances in rates, the Bank Rate technique will become a very sensitive regulator indeed. To reach this state of affairs, however, it is necessary that the Bank Rate weapon should in the past have been handled with sufficient skill and determination to give the trading community a healthy respect for the policy of the central bank; nothing succeeds like success. This happy state of affairs can be reached, however, only if the central bank is unhampered by any countervailing considerations which will restrict its freedom to pursue a policy of stabilization, such as undue concern for the budgetary effects of high interest rates.

So far, we seem to have achieved no more impressive result than the conclusion that changes in Bank Rate will sometimes induce inverse changes in the level of incomes and sometimes will not. But the underlying principle is clear. Bank Rate will fail to prevent a rise in incomes if expectations of profit nevertheless exceed the market rate of interest even after the rise. But a rise in the market rate of interest which is more than outweighed by a rise in expectations of profit is, algebraically, exactly the same thing as a *fall* in the rate of interest, the level of confidence remaining unchanged. If we define 'a rise in the rate of interest' to mean a rise in interest rates *relatively* to the general level of profit expectations, then we are entitled to say that (such) a rise in interest rates will *always* depress activity, and conversely. Similarly, manipulations of the market rate of interest will always keep the economy on an even keel if its movements exactly keep pace with changes in the level of profit expectations.[1]

Some people may be inclined to object that this way of putting things demolishes rather than reinforces the practical case for Bank Rate as a regulative instrument, since the level of business confidence fluctuates wildly between expectations of very large profits and fears of heavy loss, while even short-term interest rates move in practice within a relatively narrow range.

1. In the terminology sometimes used by economists, this is equivalent to saying that the 'equilibrium' rate of interest is one which equals the 'marginal efficiency of capital.' This is a nice concrete-sounding expression which, however, on closer examination tends to disintegrate into nothing more exact or scientific than 'the level of business confidence.'

Things are not, however, nearly as bad as this. In the first place, the 'true' market rate of interest fluctuates more widely than the recorded money rates of interest, because the fring of excluded borrowers tends to widen during an upswing in activity. Secondly, we have to ask ourselves why the business community should in fact take the bit in its teeth in the way assumed. Most frequently, the only difficulty is that a boom has already got under way and it is the resulting rise in prices which is causing abnormally high expectations of profit. If the authorities are sufficiently vigilant and resolute (and especially if they have already established a reputation for these qualities in the eyes of the business community) a rise in Bank Rate will be an extremely effective weapon; it is 'too little and too late' that will be fatal.

In saying this, however, we have done much to rebut the popular disparagement of the Bank Rate technique on the ground that, even if a high Bank Rate will check a boom, a very low rate can do little to promote rapid recovery from a depression. For a severe depression is normally the aftermath of an antecedent boom; if the authorities are alert and adroit the boom will be nipped in the bud and there will be no long drawn-out depression to terminate. If a serious depression does nevertheless occur, then, of course, credit policy will have to be supplemented by other methods of stimulating recovery which are more rapid in their action, such as deficit finance.

It is only if one believes that the level of spending will always tend to be insufficient to maintain reasonably full employment – that saving will chronically tend to outrun investments – that the Bank Rate technique must be regarded as inherently inadequate and requiring reinforcement by other measures. Before the war, this conception of a chronic deficiency of spending was very firmly entrenched in highly developed industrial countries such as Britain and the United States. But we must remember that this was a period of breakdown in international trade and, above all, in international lending, a period when the Balkanization of the world economy through piecemeal, nationalistic measures to combat the great depression had raised abnormally great impediments to the movement across national frontiers of men, goods and capital. Certainly, after twelve years of post-war inflation, the alleged danger of excessive saving appears completely unreal.

BANK RATE CHANGES SINCE 1930

Year	*Date of Change*	*Rate* %	*Year*	*Date of Change*	*Rate* %
1930	Feb. 6	4½	1955	Jan. 27	3½
	Mar. 6	4		Feb. 24	4½
	20	3½	1956	Feb. 16	5½
	May 1	3	1957	Feb. 7	5
1931	May 14	2½		Sept. 19	7
	July 23	3½	1958	Mar. 20	6
	30	4½		May 22	5½
	Sept. 21	6		June 19	5
1932	Feb. 18	5		Aug. 14	4½
	Mar. 10	4		Nov. 20	4
	17	3½			
	Apl. 21	3	1960	Jan. 21	5
	May 12	2½		June 23	6
	June 30	2		Oct. 27	5½
1939	Aug. 24	4		Dec. 8	5
	Sept. 28	3	1961	July 26	7
	Oct. 26	2		Oct. 5	6½
				Nov. 2	6
1951	Nov. 8	2½	1962	Mar. 8	5½
1952	Mar. 12	4		22	5
1953	Sep. 17	3½		Apl. 26	4½
1954	May 13	3	1963	Jan. 3	4
			1964	Feb. 27	5

CHAPTER XIII

THE BEGINNINGS OF CHEAP MONEY

THE conversion of War Loan from a 5 per cent to a 3½ per cent basis in 1932 ushered in a period of cheap money that lasted for nineteen years. Except for a brief rise to 4 per cent at the outbreak of war (reversed within a few weeks), Bank Rate stood unchanged at 2 per cent from June 1932 until November 1951. The period was marked by a fundamentally new pattern of interest rates, as will be seen from the diagram overleaf.

From 1924 until 1931 we find much the same kind of movements in rates, and of relationships between long-term and short-term rates, that one would expect under gold standard conditions, with Bank Rate oscillating between 2½ per cent and 6½ per cent, and the yield on Consols fluctuating between about 4¼ per cent and 4¾ per cent. Between 1925, the year in which we returned to the gold standard, and the end of 1928, Bank Rate varied only between 4 and 5 per cent, with a long spell at 4½ during the last twenty months of the period. With a Consols yield of about 4½ per cent, this cannot be said by any means to represent cheap money, for the desire of the authorities to lower the cost of the national debt was frustrated by the none too co-operative policies of some other central banks and by concern for our own balance of payments.

Nevertheless, these first four years of the gold standard were years of relatively good trade, with the national income in terms of money extremely stable, real wages rising and unemployment (except for the period of the general strike) ranging between the 'hard-core' level of a million and an upper limit of about 1,200,000. Similar conditions persisted into 1929. The rise in Bank Rate during that year to 6½ per cent reflected the Wall

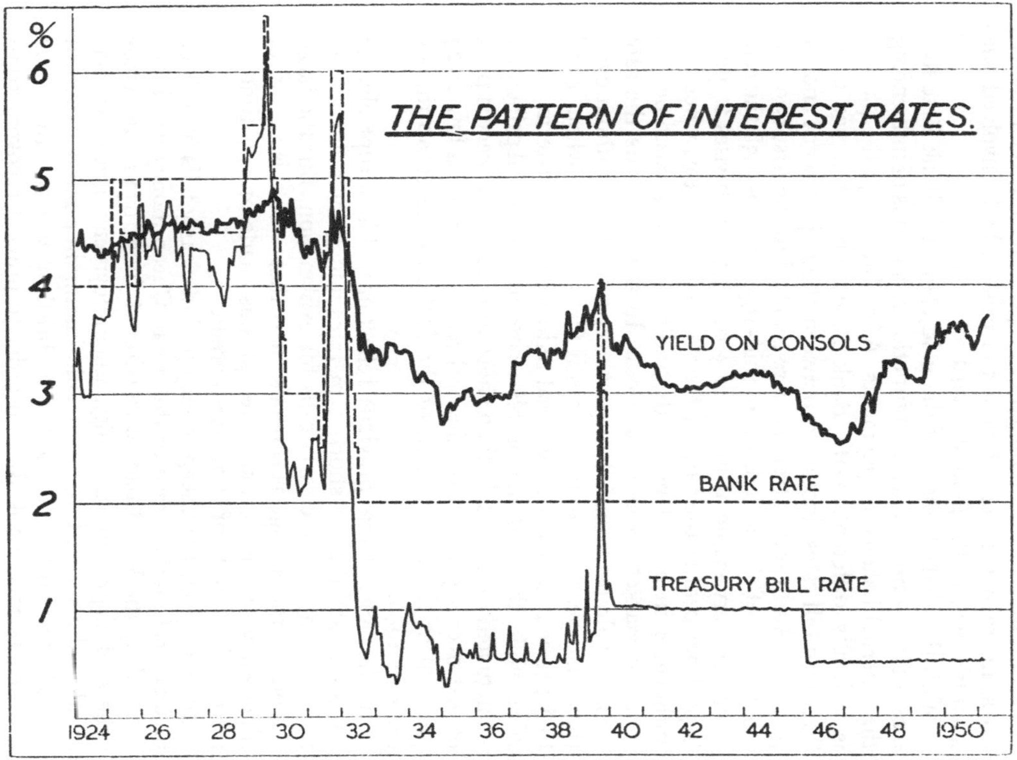
THE PATTERN OF INTEREST RATES.
%
6
5
4
3
2
1
YIELD ON CONSOLS
BANK RATE
TREASURY BILL RATE
1924
26
28
30
32
34
36
38
40
42
44
46
48
1950

Diagram 9

Street boom, and the subsequent return to 3 per cent the breaking of that boom. For a few weeks in the middle of 1931 the Bank rate was actually reduced to 2½ per cent, but then rushed up again to 6 per cent during the crisis which involved the abandonment of the gold standard.

With the abandonment of the gold standard, Bank Rate lost most of its traditional primary function as a means of influencing the external balance of payments. After June 1932 the pattern is radically different. With Bank Rate stable at 2 per cent, Treasury bill rates fluctuated between about ¼ per cent and 1¼ per cent. And these extremes were touched in the first two and a half years of the period. From mid-1935 to mid-1938 the rate remained very stable at just over ½ per cent, with rises to perhaps ¾ per cent at the turn of the year and half-year, when the authorities in accordance with tradition were accustomed to 'put the market through its paces.' In the war years the rate remained almost immobile at just over 1 per cent, without even these half-yearly movements, until October 1945, when it fell to ½ per cent as part of a general reduction in short-term rates. Meanwhile, the yield on Consols – contrary to general principles – fluctuated more widely than short-term rates, between a peak of just over 4 per cent on the outbreak of war and a low of 2½ per cent at the culmination of the Dalton ultra-cheap money drive of 1946.

In the light of our previous reflections, this abrupt change – towards stability of short-term rates and greater fluctuation in long-term rates – clearly calls for explanation. But the basic reason for the change is obvious: it is that over this period of nineteen years no serious attempt was made at any time to restrict the supply of short-term credit.

In retrospect, the cheap money period clearly falls into three phases, each in its own way abnormal. Cheap money was inaugurated by the War Loan conversion of June 1932 in an atmosphere of depression and high unemployment. Recovery was rapid in the succeeding years, culminating in a minor boom in 1937, but at no time up to the outbreak of war was there any occasion to raise Bank Rate in order to prevent recovery from developing into an inflationary boom; nor was there any necessity for high rates on balance of payments grounds, thanks to the large influx of gold as the counterpart of an influx of foreign balances. During the war itself no attempt was made to restrict the supply of credit. On the contrary, policy sought to ensure that the war effort (and in the later years all activities still left in being must be deemed of indirect if not direct assistance to the war effort) should not be impeded for lack of finance. The attempted safeguard against inflation consisted of a network of direct restraints on spending. With the relaxation or breakdown of these controls in the post-war period, and with the war-time legacy of a greatly expanded money supply, it might be thought that recourse to credit restriction could no longer be avoided. Given the very considerable volume of floating debt, however, there appeared a good case on grounds of expediency for seeking to curb inflation by the alternative method of a budget surplus. Even when this approach had manifestly failed (the achievement of a sufficiently large surplus to bring disinflation having been frustrated by constantly rising expenditure) short-term rates were left unchanged at cheap money levels notwithstanding the continuance of inflation.

While Bank Rate remained unchanged from 1932 to 1951, the size of the money supply, of course, did not. Changes took place in the level of bank deposits which did not necessarily coincide with changes in the liquidity requirements of the domestic public. In other words, variations took place in the liquidity of the system which were reflected in a rising or falling trend in gilt-edged prices.

From the chart on page 141, three broad movements can be discerned during this period. First we have a rise in the yield of Consols from under 3 per cent in 1934 to a peak of about 4 per cent touched during the early months of the war. This is explicable (a) by the fact that incomes were rising more rapidly than bank deposits during the recovery years, i.e., the income velocity of bank deposits was rising[1] and (b) the uncertainties arising out of the various political crises and finally the outbreak of war created at times an abnormal desire for liquidity (an increase in liquidity preference). During the war years, considerable additions were made to the money supply while at the same time the use of this credit was restricted by rationing

1. See p. 112 for the effects of Exchange Account finance in 1937.

and other restraints. The money supply was thus running ahead of incomes, liquidity increased and long-term interest rates gradually declined, a movement culminating in the Dalton cheap money drive of 1946 (see Chapter XV). From 1946 onwards on the other hand, incomes were expanding more rapidly than the money supply and gilt-edged prices fell.

CHAPTER XIV

DEFICIT FINANCE

THERE are only two ways in which any individual can legitimately increase his cash balance: in return for part of his current output (i.e., as the counterpart of current saving) or through the sale or mortgage of capital assets. It follows that the liquid assets of the public as a whole (the stock of money) can be increased only in the same two ways: by the sale of current output or of capital assets to the monetary authorities (who may in turn borrow from the commercial banks to finance their purchase). Hitherto, we have noted two ways in which the supply of money may be increased as the counterpart of official purchases of capital assets: namely, official purchases of (1) gold or foreign exchange, and (2) gilt-edged securities. In the present chapter we shall be concerned with an expansion in the supply of money in payment for part of the current output of the community: that is, with the problems of deficit finance, which in turn is typically war finance.

The central problem of war finance is to enable the Government to secure command of a greatly increased proportion of current output. Once the economy is fully employed, this can be done without inflation only if every increase in government expenditure is offset by an equivalent decline in private expenditure: that is, in the combined total of consumption expenditure and private capital formation. Contrary to a popular and fatal belief, that result would not be achieved if the increase in government spending were matched pound for pound by an increase in taxation, the budget remaining in balance and no recourse being made to deficit finance. The reason is that a given increase in taxation cannot be counted upon to induce an equivalent reduction in spending, for companies may reduce their allocations to reserves in order to complete capital projects or maintain dividends, and persons will cut down their saving in the hope of preventing too drastic a reduction in their standard of living. In other words, the impact on spending of any increase in taxation will be cushioned by a decline in saving, just as the springs in a car take a large part of the shocks given by bumps in the road. If the Government merely keeps its budget balanced, therefore, this will not prevent an inflationary rise in total expenditure. Complete avoidance of inflation demands that taxation should increase *more than* government expenditure.

In practice, this is a virtually impossible ideal to live up to. Taking the nation as a whole, of course, there would not be the slightest increase in the real sacrifices demanded by war if this *were* financed wholly by taxation: deficit finance can neither reduce nor postpone the deprivations which are involved. But the choice between taxation and deficit finance does affect the allocation of the financial burden between individuals. Large sections would be very hard pressed, or quite unable to meet their tax liabilities, if rates of taxation were raised too drastically at a time of rapid change, such as the outbreak of war, when millions of people are moving into the Forces and possibly suffering a severe reduction in income in the process, and many others losing their normal occupations before being absorbed into the war effort. Especially before the introduction of P.A.Y.E., moreover, a considerable time-lag could not be avoided between a rise in incomes and the collection of taxes on the additional income; and even this interval would be sufficient for an inflationary spiral to get under way.

Inevitably, therefore, war means some degree of inflation. The methods adopted for the finance of the war must be deemed successful to the extent that:

(a) a given increase in government expenditure is associated with only a small increase in the deficit;
(b) a given deficit is associated with only a small increase in personal incomes; and
(c) a given increase in incomes is associated with only a small increase in expenditure on consumption.

The problem of war finance, in other words, is essentially that of *defeating the multiplier.*[1] However drastic the increase in taxation, one would not expect this endeavour to be very successful in a free economy. If the Government relies mainly on bidding-up for resources, indeed, the process tends to end in galloping inflation. Moreover, an inflation of this traditional kind involves a double measure of social injustice: the bidding-up process results in an inflation of profits, so that the additional

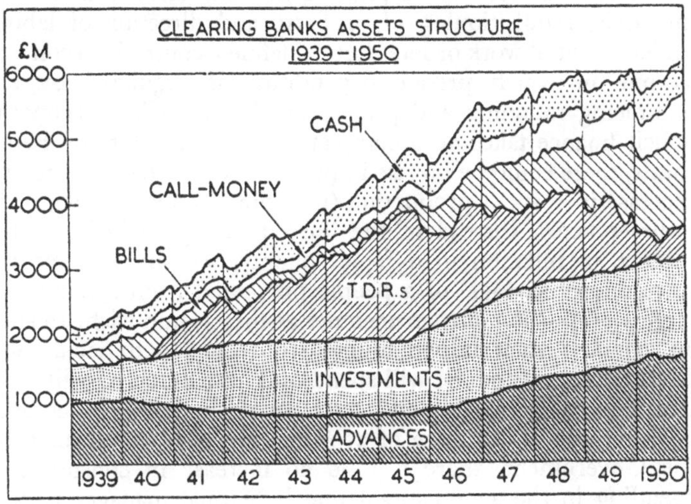

Diagram 10

national debt which is created to finance the deficit comes to rest in the hands of entrepreneurs; yet the actual sacrifices are exacted through the reduction – by rising prices – of the real purchasing power of incomes which are fixed in terms of money (e.g., pensions), or which lag behind the rise in prices. And in a profit inflation the latter will *ex hypothesi* include wage incomes.

1. An increase in spending tends to create a multiple addition to incomes, the 'multiplier' depending on the proportion of additional income which, on the average, is left unspent, e.g., if the community saves on the average one-half of any increment of money income, the multiplier (as best defined for our purposes) will be 2, if one-quarter is saved the multiplier will be 4, and so on.

In spite of belated and amateurish attempts at rationing and price control, the 1914–18 war was basically financed by a profit inflation of this kind. By contrast, it was an outstanding feature of the 1939–45 war that the allocation of resources between Government and the civil population was not left to the workings of the price mechanism and the bidding-up process. It was decided, once the framework of control had been erected, by direct restraints on spending: by rationing, price control, restriction of non-war capital formation, allocation of raw materials, requisitioning of property and direction of labour under essential work orders. Let us define a controlled economy as one in which private expenditure is regulated by all-embracing rationing and price controls. In such an economy deficit finance takes on a completely new character; by hypothesis, there could be no rise in prices except in response to any increase in costs of production (including import prices), or in indirect taxes. Instead of the 'forced savings' which are the essence of inflation in a free economy, we should have the 'involuntary savings' of a people prevented from spending as large a proportion of their incomes as they would wish. In such an economy, each individual may still seem free to decide how much of his income he will spend and how much he will save, but collectively there is no longer any such choice. Since both the supply and the price of consumption goods is decided by the Government, there can be no increase in consumption spending in the aggregate; if one individual manages to buy more unrationed goods, and so to save less, others will be able to spend less, and hence forced to save more. The consumer's deprivations will reflect themselves in queues, waiting lists and shop shortages, but there need be no *active* inflation in the sense of a rise in prices due to monetary causes; the inflationary pressures will have been suppressed by the controls, though nevertheless remaining latent.

This concept of a completely controlled economy is, of course, an abstraction and not a description of our actual war economy. In reality, the framework of control took some time to erect. Although there was considerable slack in the economy when war broke out, the initial burst of inflation, coupled with a rise in import costs, was sufficient to cause a sharp rise in prices, which in the first eighteen months or so rose somewhat ahead of wage rates (see Diagram 11). Thereafter the rise in prices was checked by rationing, price control and subsidies. But a wages spiral had been started and – given our traditional methods of wage negotiation and the state of over-full employ-

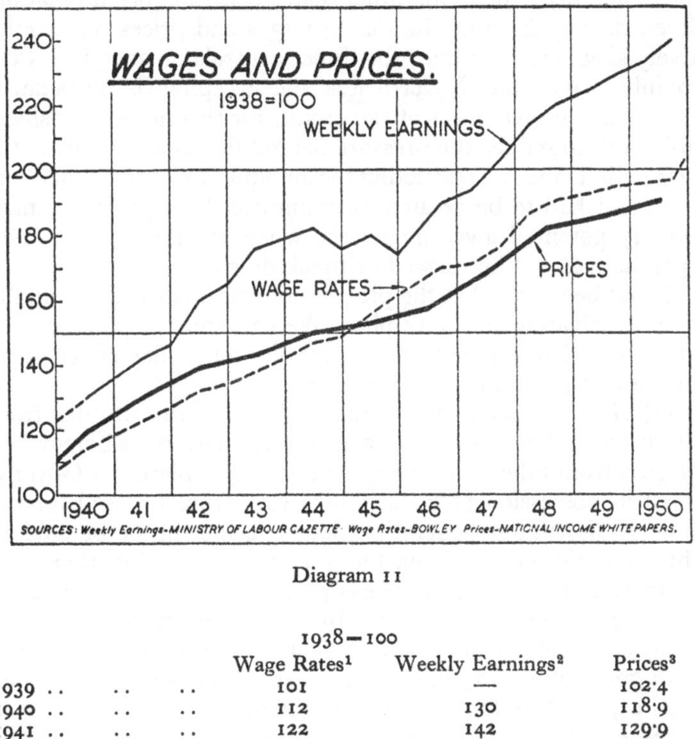

Diagram 11

1938—100

	Wage Rates[1]	Weekly Earnings[2]	Prices[3]
1939	101	—	102·4
1940	112	130	118·9
1941	122	142	129·9
1942	131	160	138·9
1943	138	176	143·2
1944	146	181	149·6
1945	154	180	153·0
1946	167	190	158·1
1947	175	203	169·2
1948	188	220	180·2
1949	193½	229	186·6
1950	197	240	191·1

1. London and Cambridge Economic Service. 2. Ministry of Labour. 3. National Income White Papers.

ment maintained not only during the war but almost continuously ever since – has not yet been halted. After 1941 indeed, the active inflation in the form of rising prices (with the resulting hardships for groups with fixed or lagging money incomes), must be ascribed very largely to this wages spiral. It has been a cost and price inflation, rather than a price and profit inflation. Even during the war, the rise in wages and prices was a relatively slow one. For that, the direct controls on spending were mainly responsible. Nevertheless, the sweeping rise in taxation must also be given part of the credit, for this helped considerably both to reduce the pressure behind the controls during the war period, and, by restricting the amount of additional national debt that had to be created, to minimize the suppressed inflationary potential awaiting release whenever the controls over spending should be relaxed or break down.

It has been said that the problem of war finance is essentially one of defeating the multiplier. We can enumerate a number of factors that will help to reduce the multiplier effect of an increase in government expenditure:

(1) *An increased import surplus.* Whether this results from drafts on gold or other external assets, from overseas borrowing, or gifts from other countries, the effect is to place the Government in possession of goods which can either be used for the war effort without generating domestic income or be sold to the domestic public. From the monetary viewpoint, therefore, an increased import surplus has precisely the same effect as an increase in taxation or saving.[1] In tracing the effects of government spending on domestic incomes, we are concerned only with government expenditure requiring domestic finance (i.e., total expenditure less overseas borrowing).

(2) *A reduction in private capital formation.* In the early war years this was a useful offset to the expansion in government expenditure. So far from there being any further net additions to the physical capital of the private sector, expenditure on renewals and replacements fell below the level needed to replace the capital used up during the year. On the other hand, companies continued to make current provision for amortization, even though the greater part of this money could not be spent

1. See pages 111–12.

at the time, and these unspent depreciation allowances were available to finance government spending. It is not a deficit as such which generates additional income, but an increase in 'investment' as a whole, i.e., an increase in the combined total of domestic capital formation and the public deficit requiring finance from domestic saving.[1]

(3) *An increase in taxation* will, of course, reduce the multiplier effect of government spending, provided that the taxation has its counterpart in a curtailment of private spending and not of private saving. It is only deficit spending which tends directly to generate additional income.

(4) *Physical controls*, if efficient and all-embracing, will ensure that additional income cannot be spent.

If the economy is fully extended, if private capital formation has been reduced to a minimum and there is no increase in the external deficit, any increase in the government deficit requiring finance from domestic saving will call for an equivalent reduction in consumption expenditure at factor cost if inflation is to be avoided; for in those conditions any increase in public expenditure involves the diversion to the public sector of resources formerly employed in producing consumers' goods. Provided that any rise in prices is prevented by the physical controls, consumption expenditure will *automatically* decline in proportion to the decline in the available supply of consumers' goods; which means that a corresponding amount of income will be left unspent, i.e., that increased government spending will automatically generate an equivalent increase in saving.

Even in the later war years, we did not have a fully controlled economy as defined above. The most that the controls achieved was to *damp down* the amount of spending out of additional income generated by deficit spending, for a narrow fringe of inessentials remained uncontrolled and prices in general had to be raised to allow for antecedent rises in costs. We can

1. It should be noted that transfers to private capital accounts, such as war damage compensation or E.P.T. refunds, do not require to be financed by current saving. In effect, the Government hands over government securities which the beneficiary holds as a capital asset. If the securities are sold and the proceeds used for expenditure on capital formation, then this expenditure will, of course, need to be financed from current saving; but the original paper transaction will not.

appraise the success of the methods of finance employed by reference to what we shall call the 'inflation factor' in consumption expenditure. From the National Income White Papers we know how the available supply of consumption goods varied from year to year. The 'inflation factor' for any year represents any excess of consumption spending (at factor cost) over the value of the available supply of consumption goods as measured at the prices ruling in the previous year.[1]

The period 1938 to 1948 may be divided into three phases, whose characteristics from the monetary viewpoint are summarized in the following table:

	Changes between:		
	1938 and 1943	1943 and 1946	1946 and 1948
	£m	£m	£m
(1) Government expenditure requiring domestic finance	+ 4,449	− 1,893	−578
(2) Public deficit requiring finance from private saving	+ 1,738	− 1,651	−825
(3) Investment requiring finance from personal saving	+ 1,209	− 630	−467
(4) Personal income	+ 2,819	+ 755	+880
(5) Spendable income	+ 2,175	+ 736	+786
(6) Consumption at factor cost ..	+ 456	+ 1,296	+934
(7) Average 'inflation factor' for period	223	141	334
	%	%	%
(8) Average annual rise in consumption goods prices at factor cost ..	6¼	3–4½	8¼

By 1943 the mobilization of the economy for a total war effort had virtually been completed. The inflationary impact of the enormous increase in government expenditure had been damped down by the absorption of resources unemployed at the outbreak of war, by the curtailment of private capital formation, by a sweeping rise in taxation, and by the erection of a system of physical restraints on spending very nearly equivalent to the combination of universal rationing with universal price control. Comparing 1943 with 1938, an increase of £4,449 millions in

1. It should not be concluded that inflation would have been halted if only taxation and saving could have been increased by the amount of the 'inflation factor'. Such an increase would still have meant a state of over-full employment, and therefore a continuance of the wages spiral.

government expenditure requiring domestic finance was thus accomplished with a rise of only £2,819 millions in personal incomes, and of no more than £456 millions in consumption at factor cost. Since the available supply of consumption goods had been sharply reduced, however, this small increase in consumption expenditure reflects a fair amount of active inflation, though the average annual rise of 6¼ per cent in consumption goods prices over the five-year period is heavily weighted by the sharp advance in 1940.

Our second period, lasting until the end of 1946, includes the greater part of the phase of economic demobilization. Government expenditure requiring domestic finance declined on balance by nearly £1,900 millions, but as this decline was largely offset by the revival of private capital formation the demands on personal saving were reduced only by £630 millions. Even so, one might *a priori* have expected such a decline in investment to make it possible to halt the rise in personal income. The continued expansion can probably be attributed to two main factors. First, the removal at the end of hostilities of essential work orders, followed by some bidding-up for labour and an aggravation of the wages spiral. Secondly, some weakening of the effectiveness of the direct controls over spending, whose extreme efficiency during the war was perhaps attributable less to vigilant administration than to such factors as the black-out, the negligible supply of goods other than basic essentials, and, above all, to patriotic motives. Whether and to what extent the inflation of 1946 was aggravated by a third factor, namely, Mr. Dalton's cheap money drive, is a matter for discussion. In any case, consumption expenditure and capital formation together rose more rapidly than government expenditure was declining. However, in 1946 the actual supply of consumers' goods was substantially increased, so that the large rise in consumption expenditure at factor cost was attributable only in a minor degree to rising prices.

In the two succeeding years the economic background – declining investment more than offset by rising consumer spending – was similar to that of 1946, but in spite of the reduced demands on private saving and an extremely large import surplus the pace of active inflation was sharply accelerated. Indeed, 1947 ranks second only to 1940 as a year of inflation. Yet whereas 1940 was a year of hasty mobilization, rapidly mounting war expenditure and relatively low taxation, the circumstances of 1947 were in most respects precisely the opposite: war expenditure tailing off sharply, large numbers of people returning from the Forces to civilian production, and taxation maintained virtually at peak war levels. It is true that 1947, like 1940, saw a sharp rise in import prices, but it is arguable how far that should be reckoned as an independent source of inflationary pressure. As such, a rise in import prices will actually benefit the budgetary position. If on balance it nevertheless has an inflationary effect, this is due to the maintenance (either as a deliberate act of policy or through a failure of financial policy) of a state of over-full employment in which a wages spiral cannot be resisted. This leaves no other choice than to pass on the higher import prices to the consumer and so accelerate the wages spiral, or to avoid this result at the cost of increased subsidies. That particular problem presented itself in an even more acute form with the upward leap in world commodity prices after the outbreak of war in Korea, which brought a fresh bout of inflation after the relative stability achieved, with the help of large budget surpluses and a rigorous wage freeze policy, in 1949 and the first half of 1950.

So much for the progress of inflation during the war and early post-war years and the varying success of the efforts to suppress or halt it. What part has the monetary mechanism to play in all this? In a free economy, of course, expansion of the money stock can be regarded as the operative factor in inflation. In the first instance, the Government creates additional money (or activates formerly idle money) in order to outbid the demands of the private sector and so divert resources to the war effort. In the next stage, the private sector uses this additional money in an attempt to outbid the Government and restore its command over resources, so that a cumulative creation of new money will become necessary if the Government is to maintain, let alone increase further, its share of the total resources available. None of this, clearly, applies to a completely controlled economy, in our sense of an economy in which spending is regulated by all-embracing and efficient direct controls. It is quite evident that in such an economy the size of the money stock cannot influence the level of spending. Instead, we have to reverse our approach entirely and ask what factors, the level of total expenditure being given, will in such an economy govern the size of the money stock.

Before attempting to answer this question we must take account of two basic changes in the banking and monetary situations as compared with the normal pre-war position, which together operated to prevent pyramiding by the banks on the basis of additional liquid assets. Early in the war the Chancellor, through the Bank of England, requested the banks on the one hand to refrain from granting loans for non-essential purposes, in particular the finance of luxury industries or loans to individuals, and on the other hand to ensure as far as possible that production essential to the war effort should not be impeded for lack of finance.[1] Hence, there could be no question of an excess of liquid assets leading to any expansion of advances over and above that demanded for the efficient conduct of the war economy.

There remained the possibility that the banks, if they were to follow the conventional rules concerning their assets structure, might utilize surplus liquid assets to increase their investments portfolio. If the additional securities were supplied by the authorities, this could not have caused any expansion in bank deposits. It was, however, ruled out in any event by the introduction of Treasury deposit receipts. Unlike Treasury bills, these were not a negotiable security but were issued to a particular bank. And whereas the banks are at least nominally free to decide what volume of Treasury bills they will buy from the discount market, or enable the discount market itself to finance with bank money, the system of issue of Treasury deposit receipts was such that each bank was informed how many Treasury deposit receipts it was expected to take up each week. This enabled the authorities to withdraw cash from the banks on whatever scale they desired. If the T.D.R. call was fixed high enough, the banks would have no surplus liquid assets left. Throughout the war years, Treasury deposit receipts did in fact provide the counterpart for the great bulk of the

1. See Appendix.

additional bank credit. The combined total of the money market assets, investments and advances showed little increase; and to the extent that the banks did add to their combined holdings of these four main pre-war assets this must be presumed to have had the tacit approval of the authorities.

The effect of these safeguards against pyramiding, clearly, is that the level of bank liquidity ceased to have any causal significance. Just as, in war conditions, it is the flow of spending which largely governs the size of the money stock, and not conversely, so the normal relationship between liquid assets and the volume of deposits is reversed. Deposits are determined by the amount which the government borrow through the banking system and their level decides what cash reserves and liquid assets the banks will need to maintain the conventional ratios.

One of the major factors governing the level of deposits, in turn, arises out of the second of our basic changes: namely, the freedom accorded to the public by the system of 'tap' issues – i.e., securities continuously on offer for a period[1] – to decide how much of its total savings it would hold in the form of bank deposits and other liquid assets, and how much in the form of holdings of long-term securities. In pre-war days before the invention of cheap money policies, it was axiomatic, as we have seen, that the actions of the public could in no way affect the volume of credit. Once a given volume of deposits had been created, an attempt by the public to exchange out of deposits into goods would merely drive up prices, without in fact reducing the *volume* of credit, while in the same way an attempt to exchange out of deposits into securities would merely drive up

1. During the war of 1914–18 the more usual practice was to make periodical offers of loans for subscription on a particular day. This technique was adopted only once during the 1939–45 war, with the floating of the 3 per cent War Loan on March 5th, 1940. The contrast with the tap system is more apparent than real, for, regardless of the financial technique adopted for attracting savings into a particular form, saving itself is a continuous process. Thus, although several hundred millions pounds may be subscribed to a new loan in a few hours, the actual transfer of funds to the authorities would normally be spread over a longish period by the operations of the Departments. It is normal practice for the Departments to 'clear the decks' in anticipation of a new issue, i.e., gradually to dispose of their holdings of existing securities and to hold the proceeds in liquid form, typically in tap bills. When the new issue is floated, the Departments can thus take up a large slice and peddle it out gradually to the public as savings accumulate.

the price of securities. Under war conditions, however, the public had for the greater part of the time complete freedom to exchange out of deposits into the various 'tap' issues almost continuously on offer, and were of course encouraged to do so by all the blandishments of the savings movement. The main function of the savings movement, indeed, was not to generate savings, for that was accomplished primarily by the direct controls over spending, but to ensure that savings were invested in a relatively long-term and stable form instead of being held in the highly volatile form of bank deposits and other liquid assets, offering a constant temptation to spending if the controls should ultimately be relaxed or become ineffective.[1]

The factors which led the public to continue to hold part of their assets in liquid form, rather than to invest in the 'tap' issues for the sake of the interest return, were of course those which normally constitute the demand for money. With some over-simplification, we can divide bank deposits into two fundamental categories: those held as a provision against contingencies of various kinds whose amount is closely related to the level of incomes and prices; and those which represent liquid savings awaiting investment. Normally, the two categories correspond very roughly to the division between current and deposit accounts, but the incentive promptly to transfer to

1. The tap issues included (1) National Savings Certificates and Defence Bonds, designed to appeal primarily to the small investor, offering a higher return than marketable securities of comparable life and therefore made available only in limited amounts to any one individual; (2) deposits in the Post Office and Trustee Savings Banks, also designed primarily for the small saver, offering since 1931 a higher return than the commercial banks could allow and also restricted as to amount; (3) relatively short-dated National War Bonds and longer-term Savings Bonds, marketable securities intended for the large saver and institutional investor; and (4), from late 1941 onwards, tax reserve certificates which could be used for the payment of taxes within two years of issue.

The return on National Savings Certificates takes the form of capital appreciation over a period and in the case of the initial issues, at any rate, was equivalent to a relatively high annual interest payment subject to tax. Tax reserve certificates, offering a small but tax-free return, were particularly attractive to very large investors paying extremely high rates of taxation on their marginal income or to companies subject to 100 per cent Excess Profits Tax. But all the tap issues offered some annual return, whereas the rates obtainable on bank balances were at all times low, and after October 1945 limited to ½ per cent on deposit accounts, with no interest payment at all on current accounts.

deposit account any balances not regarded as necessary for current purposes becomes negligible when deposit rate falls to extremely low levels.

One of the main factors governing the use of bank balances as a repository for liquid savings is uncertainty about the future course of security prices. Other things equal, savings will flow more freely out of bank deposits into tap issues if security prices are expected to remain stable or rise, and conversely. As it happens, the framework of deficit finance in a controlled economy is particularly well adapted to the maintenance of low and gradually declining interest rates. Competition for savings on the part of borrowers other than the Government is reduced to an indispensable minimum by the restraints on private capital formation. To create an abundance of liquid assets can have no *immediate* inflationary consequences, thanks to the physical controls; and the system of tap issues itself operates as a kind of thermostatic control to prevent a rise in interest rates or, within limits, actually to reduce them. Let us suppose that for a period the public become unwilling to invest in the currently available tap issues, so that the flow of subscriptions falls off. It follows that the Government will be compelled to finance a correspondingly greater part of its current requirements by borrowing through the banking system. Bank deposits will expand (as a counterpart of the accumulating savings generated by the deficit spending), the liquidity of the public will gradually increase and after a time the flow of subscriptions to the tap issues will be resumed.

This mechanism clearly makes it possible, up to a point, to float successive tap issues on terms progressively more favourable to the borrower. At first, the public may be inclined to doubt whether a new issue on the lower yield basis will maintain its value, but these doubts are likely gradually to evaporate as the accumulating funds exert an upward pressure on the price level of existing securities, rendering the tap issues once again attractive by comparison with alternative avenues of investment. The psychological effectiveness of this process will be enhanced if the authorities leave an interval, as they sometimes did, between the closing of the tap for one issue and the announcement of its successor.

We are now in a position to trace the monetary effects of deficit finance in a fully controlled economy. For the sake of simplicity, we may conceive the complicated processes involved as taking place in three stages, though in practice they will be taking place simultaneously:

(1) We will suppose that in the first period the Government finances a deficit of £100 millions by borrowing from the Bank of England. The result is a parallel expansion of £100 millions in bank cash and bank deposits. Saving also rises by £100 millions and income by an amount depending on the size of the multiplier.

(2) In the second stage we will suppose that the additional bank cash is absorbed by an issue of Treasury deposit receipts and/or Treasury bills, except for that part of the additional cash which is needed to support the increase in deposits, i.e., if the cash ratio is 8 per cent, then £8 millions of the additional cash reserves will be left in existence and £92 millions withdrawn by an issue of Treasury deposit receipts and/or Treasury bills, the proceeds of this issue being used to repay the greater part of the initial borrowing from the Bank of England (leaving the Banking Department's assets and liabilities £8 millions higher than at the outset). At this stage, however, the public will still be holding the whole of its additional £100 millions of savings in the form of bank deposits. Admittedly, the demand for bank deposits will probably have been increased by the rise in incomes, but the public may well be prepared to surrender a larger proportion of the additional deposits in exchange for securities.

(3) Let us suppose that it decides to subscribe £50 millions to the currently available tap issue and that of this sum the banks, in effect, transfer £4 millions to the authorities in the form of cash and the remaining £46 millions by the encashment of Treasury deposit receipts. The net result is that the Government will have financed its deficit of £100 millions as to £4 millions by borrowing from the Bank of England (having its counterpart in an addition to bank cash reserves), as to £46 millions by the issue of Treasury deposit receipts to the banks, and/or an increase in the tender Treasury bill issue, and as to £50 millions by the sale of securities to the public.

There is obviously no fixed relationship between the size of a deficit and the amount of credit expansion which is involved in its finance. In the extreme case, a large deficit could be financed without any permanent addition to bank deposits at all, and yet without any upward pressure on interest rates. This will be the case if the deficit spending does not generate additional income, i.e., if the necessary savings are made available – spontaneously or through the action of the controls – out of existing incomes. Even if the deficit does generate a rise in incomes, there need still be no enduring expansion of credit if the public should wish to hold a smaller proportion of its savings in liquid form. On either of these assumptions, the whole of the additional deposits (created by the finance of the deficit through the banking system in the first instance) can be drained off into securities issued to the public, without the need to offer the incentive of higher interest rates. On the other hand, even a small deficit will be accompanied by a large expansion of credit if (a) it generates a large increase in income, or (b) there is an increase in the 'liquidity preference' of the public and it is sought to prevent interest rates from rising.

It is, of course, implicit in this analysis that savings which the public continues to hold in liquid form are neither more nor less 'genuine' than those which ultimately find their way into securities. Suggestions to the contrary are sometimes seen: e.g., 'bank deposits today do not represent the accumulated savings of the public, they have been created overwhelmingly by the Government itself.'[1] But the specific savings securities are also created by the Government itself, as, indeed, is an addition to the national debt in any form (and the additional deposits merely represent the counterpart of debt held by the banking system but belonging, in the last analysis, mainly to the depositors). The function of the banking system as the initial medium of deficit finance does not prevent it from being also a repository of savings. We may perhaps best view the whole process of deficit finance in the following terms: The private sector of the economy has transferred either capital assets or part of its current output to the Government in exchange for paper claims

1. The Prevention of General Unemployment. Fabian Pamphlet (Research Series, No. 79).

of various kinds. Some of these claims it chooses to take up directly and hold for its own account. The remainder are in effect transferred to the banking system in exchange for an equivalent claim on the banks, which on the one hand become entitled to the payment of interest on the new Government securities, and on the other hand agree to perform banking services for the holders of the new deposits.

CHAPTER XV

ULTRA-CHEAP MONEY

UNDER the tap issue system that we studied in the last chapter, the public were free at all times to exchange out of bank deposits into securities. The essence of a cheap money policy is precisely the opposite: that the public is free at all times to exchange out of securities into bank deposits; for a really rigid policy of stabilizing the long-term rate of interest at any level acts as a guarantee that holders of securities of any nominal life will be able to turn these into cash at any time without having to incur any risk of serious capital loss.

Both a tap issue system and a cheap money policy involve a renunciation by the authorities of any control over the volume of credit, leaving this to be determined by the liquidity preference of the public. In the former case, the renunciation is a passive one. So long as they are accepting subscriptions to a tap issue available on the stated terms, the authorities are renouncing any attempt to accelerate the flow of savings out of bank deposits into securities by the offer of more tempting rates of interest. Unless morally committed to prevent any rise in interest rates above those offered on the current tap issue, they can, however, embark on a policy of active credit restriction at any time. By committing themselves to a cheap money policy, on the other hand, the authorities not only rule out any positive recourse to restriction of credit. They also pledge themselves in advance actually to inflate bank credit on any scale that may be needed to meet the wishes of the public if at any time the latter desires to disgorge the securities it has taken up in the past and to hold liquid assets in their stead.

Given a completely controlled economy this will not, as we have seen, have any *immediate* inflationary consequences, though it may well postpone, perhaps indefinitely, the possibility of removing the controls without causing an inflationary rise in prices. If the economy is not completely controlled, on the other hand, the inflationary consequences will not even be held in suspense.

Moreover, they will be far more drastic than is often realized. For the inflationary effect of a cheap money policy is not to be measured by any actual expansion of credit which the implementation of the policy may entail. Even though the public may be perfectly willing for a time to retain the stock of securities it has taken up, so that there is no need to expand bank credit in order to absorb offerings, a pledge that interest rates will never be allowed to rise has the effect of converting all government securities, *regardless of maturity dates*, into the equivalent of cash at their current market values, rendering maturity dates meaningless.

Even in normal conditions, of course, gilt-edged securities constitute a *secondary* liquid asset, so that an expansion in national debt (relative to the national income) is inflationary in tendency. But in the absence of a cheap money policy a concerted attempt to convert gilt-edged holdings into cash will merely depress their value. Given a rigid cheap money policy, however, the possession even of a nominally 'irredeemable' stock confers as certain a claim to cash as the possession of a bank balance of equivalent value. To adopt such a policy on the morrow of a great war – when vast amounts of capital have been destroyed, when consumers have been suffering deprivations for years, and when the stock of money is already abnormally high by comparison with the national income – could, if it were persisted in, have only two outcomes: rampant inflation or the indefinite maintenance of totalitarian controls.

Fortunately, no cheap money policy can in practice be quite as thorough-going as its sponsors would like to imply, and that for two reasons, one practical and one logical. The practical reason is that not even a Government can give assurances which are 100 per cent valid and convincing about the course of events even in the relatively near future, much less for decades ahead. Hence a minority of investors will always harbour some doubts whether, let us say, a 2½ per cent irredeemable stock *will never at any time* fall below par value. Secondly, the very concept of a rigid cheap money policy hides an inherent contradiction. For if any government could irrevocably commit not only itself, but its successors *in perpetuo*, to prevent gilt-edged ever falling below their current prices, this would, as we have seen, make all securities of any nominal maturity date the equivalent of cash. It must thereby render the payment of interest rates graded according to the nominal life of the bonds an absurdity, and so remove all justification for the payment of any rate of interest at all in excess of that obtainable on bank deposits.

Let us see how this works out. We will suppose: (1) that the banks allow no interest on current accounts and ½ per cent on deposit accounts, and (2) that the authorities are committed for all time to stabilize the long-term rate of interest at the current level, which we will assume to be 3 per cent. Securities bearing interest at 3 per cent will never fall below par, and holders will be able at all times to sell them instantly at face value. There will no longer be any gain in liquidity (as distinct from convenience in making payments) from the holding of a bank balance, offering at the most ½ per cent, rather than a security yielding 3 per cent, so that the owners of a large proportion of the bank deposits in existence will wish to exchange them for securities. If it were official policy to prevent rates falling as well as rising, the authorities will have to issue additional 'long-term' securities bearing interest at 3 per cent in exchange for all the bank deposits in existence other than pure 'convenience-balances.'[1] In other words, the net result of the

1. The balances that would flow into securities are those which represent 'savings' in liquid form. These 'savings deposits' may for some purposes be approximately identified with deposit accounts, but in an era of low interest rates they undoubtedly include also large sums held on current account. If the 3 per cent securities were not merely a completely liquid asset, but also a perfect substitute for bank deposits as a medium of payment, there is no reason why any balances should be left with the banks at all; but that would only be the case if the securities were perfectly divisible (i.e., available in the same denominations as currency, including shillings and pence), and could be used for making payments with no greater risk or cost than that involved in the making of payments by cheque. Failing those qualities it would pay holders to lodge securities with the banks, sacrificing interest and, if necessary, paying bank charges into the bargain, in order to secure the safety and convenience of a 'checking' account. That is, of course, the basic reason why the banking system came into existence in the first place; if banks did not exist it would be necessary to invent them.

'cheap money' policy would be to *raise* the cost of the national debt, since the rate appropriate to long-term securities held by the public would have to be paid on that part of the debt formerly held by the banks as the counterpart of savings balances and bearing interest at much less than the 'long-term 'rate.[1]

Obviously, this is too absurd to contemplate. The authorities would clearly adopt the opposite course of *reducing* their fixed long-term rate to equality with the rate obtainable on bank deposits; for the risk having been taken out of holding securities, there would be no point in pegging the 'long-term' rate (now a complete misnomer) at any higher level. Things which are equal to the same thing must be equal to each other.

It may be argued that there are times of depression and mass unemployment when inflation is a very academic threat, and that in such a situation it might be a very good thing indeed to push the long-term rate down to say, 1 per cent – provided the authorities were ready promptly to mop up the surplus cash and raise interest rates again if the stimulus to spending afforded by virtually costless long-term credit should provoke an inflationary boom. But this argument, too, contains an obvious contradiction. If it were evident to investors that the ultra-cheap money policy would in fact be abandoned and reversed at the first sign of inflation, then the long-term rate could never fall to 1 per cent in the first instance. In taking up long-term securities, investors have to judge what the average long-term rate is going to be over a long period ahead; it is impossible to issue securities on an interest basis which investors judge to be lower than this long-term 'norm'.

Let us suppose that investors believe the 'norm' to be 3 per cent, the actual yield ruling in the market, and that the Government seeks to drive the rate down to 1 per cent. As a first step it announces that the market will be supported on a 2 per cent basis. This would be equivalent to offering to buy irredeemable 3 per cent securities[2] at 150, or 50 per cent more than the price

1. If the banks were fully extended, advances would also have to be liquidated as a result of the shrinkage in deposits and be replaced by finance through other channels.

2. If any such existed; 2½ per cent Consols, though normally described as irredeemable because they have no fixed redemption date, are of course redeemable at the Government's option at par.

which investors regard as the long-term average. Unless investors radically revise these expectations about future prices, there will be a rush to sell all existing securities in order to take advantage of the Government's generous offer; which means that in order to establish the 2 per cent rate the authorities may have literally to convert all long-term securities into bank deposits.

But there is obviously some limit to the extent to which investors can be induced to revise upwards their views about the future 'norm' of security prices. Virtual abolition of the long-term rate is in fact possible only if investors can be persuaded that not only the existing government but all future governments have irrevocably renounced the weapon of higher interest rates as a means of combatting inflation. This in turn would be feasible only if they had at their disposal some alternative means of controlling expenditure; and the only effective alternative is in fact universal rationing by means of physical controls. It follows that the elimination of the long-term rate (Keynes' 'euthanasia of the rentier') is conceivable only in two kinds of economy: either a completely totalitarian régime, or one so stagnant that even cost-free long-term capital will not suffice to bring about full employment.

It may be objected that we arrived at this *reductio ad absurdum* only by making the unreal assumption that official policy aimed at fixing the rate at a definite level and preventing it from falling as well as rising. Let us see what follows from the more realistic assumption that the 3 per cent rate is merely a 'support level', a maximum but not a minimum. In this event the authorities will not increase the supply of securities to satisfy a buying pressure. Gilt-edged prices will therefore rise above the support level, with two important consequences:

(1) A buyer of securities will now obtain a yield of somewhat *less than* 3 per cent, and

(2) He will be incurring a risk of capital loss in paying a price above that at which the authorities are certain to support the market.

At some point, this decline in yield coupled with increasing risk will make it no longer attractive to exchange out of bank deposits into securities. A position of equilibrium will be reached; a structure of interest rates will be established which serves to equate the attractiveness of bank deposits and long-term securities, thereby determining the proportions in which the public distribute their total assets as between cash and securities.

This is, of course, the normal function of interest rates. What, then, if changed by the adoption of cheap money policies? Only this: a market free from government intervention will assess the risks involved in holding long-term securities by reference to its own views about the future 'norm' of prices. Given a cheap money policy, this concept of a norm is modified by the express or implied undertaking of the authorities to support the market at a given level; or, more accurately, this undertaking becomes one factor to be taken into account by the market in assessing the long-term norm of prices. That the importance attached to such governmental assurances may easily be exaggerated is only too evident from the course of prices since the flotation of the 2½ per cent Treasury Stock, subscribers to which saw the value of their investment depreciate by over 30 per cent within three years, a loss equivalent of some 20 years' net return on the security to a holder subject to income tax at the standard rate.[1]

It will not have escaped notice that our analysis seems to imply that deposit rate, and therefore the structure of short-term rates as a whole, will normally be lower than the long-term rate. Yet, as we have already seen, it is not unusual for short-term rates to rise above the yield on Consols. There is not necessarily any inconsistency in this. Periods of very dear short money were normally of quite short duration, and were expected to be so. Some holders of long-term securities may sell them in order to take advantage of the temporarily higher return on risk-free liquid assets; but such selling will rapidly send gilt-edged prices below what is regarded as the long-term norm. Holders are thus offered the prospect of capital gains when securities should again recover to the normal level, and this prospective appreciation must be offset against the higher interest return to be obtained for a short period on bank deposits.

1. In January 1962 this stock was quoted around 38.

This is, indeed, the factor which accounts for the relative stability of the long-term interest rate side by side with highly volatile short-term rates.

If at times the authorities are paying higher interest rates on Treasury bills than the current yield on Consols, however, it may be asked why they do not take advantage of such conditions to fund Treasury bills by the issue of a long-term security. Very similar considerations apply. Though highly stable, long-term rates will usually be *somewhat* higher during a period of very dear short money than at other times. To fund Treasury bills at such a time would tend to drive the gilt-edged rate still higher, and the authorities would be committing themselves to pay this relatively unfavourable long-term rate for an extensive period, so losing the opportunity of securing more favourable terms by postponing the funding operation for a short period.

This in turn may seem to imply that any funding of deposits is most likely to take place during a depression, when the authorities, so far from draining off liquid assets into securities, ought to be increasing the supply of liquid assets in order to stimulate spending. Such a danger may exist. In practice, the best tactics would seem to be first to support gilt-edged at rising prices, so enhancing the value and liquidity of the public's security holdings, and to fund deposits when this enhanced liquidity, at low long-term rates of interest, is beginning to promote recovery. The liquidity of the public has to be measured not merely by the level of actually existing bank deposits, but by the level of bank deposits taken in conjunction with the level of the public's secondary liquid assets (i.e., overdraft limits and holdings of securities regarded as capable of realization without appreciable loss at any time).

To sum up: in the management of long-term rates, as of short, nothing succeeds like success. A really determined cheap money undertaking, accepted at face value by the market, acts as a guarantee against serious losses on long-term securities. It renders these much more nearly the equivalent of cash and is thus tantamount, in its effects on the monetary situation, to a substantial addition to bank deposits, even if no actual credit expansion is required to implement the policy. To adopt such a policy in a potentially inflationary situation is thus calculated to promote actual inflation which, in even a partially free economy, can be checked only by a rise in interest rates, inflicting severe losses on investors who have bought in reliance on the official assurances of continued cheap money. All this must clearly weaken the effectiveness of such assurances in the future, and thus destroy the usefulness of a cheap money policy when required for its legitimate purpose of combating depression. It is not by imposing on the gullibility of the public and by clever manipulation of Departmental funds, but only by promoting stable monetary conditions and keeping the economy on an even keel for long periods, that the authorities can hope to bring about a gradual but lasting fall in the long-term rate. Any such decline must reflect a secular lessening of the risks inherent in long-term investment.

It is true that capital formation tends to proceed by fits and starts, with periods of stagnation in between. But, as we have seen, it is not a very promising line of policy to seek to combat depression by artifically depressing the long-term rate during periods of stagnation; for the inevitable reversal of this movement during the next boom must inflict losses on investors who, once bitten, will be twice shy thereafter. So far as the long-term rate is concerned, governments can more usefully assist: (1) by running a deficit (preferably the result of tax remissions and not of increased expenditure) when private capital formation is at a low ebb *and* a surplus when private investment is booming; (2) by undertaking to support the gilt-edged market, and by reducing risks in other ways (e.g., by guarantees of various kinds), when it is necessary to stimulate spending *and* withdrawing these assurances if inflation threatens.

CHAPTER XVI

THE RETURN OF BANK RATE

FROM the viewpoint of monetary policy, November 1951 is clearly an important milestone. Up to that point, Bank Rate remained unchanged at the 2 per cent level first established nineteen years earlier.[1] Moreover, the authorities had abandoned any attempt to pursue an active credit policy. Stringent conditions in the money market were averted by the willingness of the special buyer always to purchase bills at around ½ per cent, so that the cash reserves needed to support any increase in bank deposits were made available without forcing the discount market into the Bank, and indeed without any rise in short-term rates at all. Although we had come out of the war with a money supply already abnormally large in relation to incomes, substantial additions were in fact made to bank deposits in 1946 (connected with the cheap money drive) and again in the early months of 1948.[2]

Once the drive to force down long-term interest rates had been abandoned, however, the supply of money was no longer left to be determined by the preferences of the public as between cash and securities. And in spite of the ½ per cent money tap, two influences were in operation to place some restraint upon the supply of money. The first of these was the retention of the directives concerning bank lending introduced early in the war.[3] While advances showed some recovery from the wartime level, they remained abnormally low in relation both to deposits and to the level of incomes.[4] In the circumstances this undoubtedly helped to place a brake upon the growth of deposits, since the

1. See table page 139. 2. See Diagrams 13 and 14. 3. See Appendix.
4. See Diagram 15.

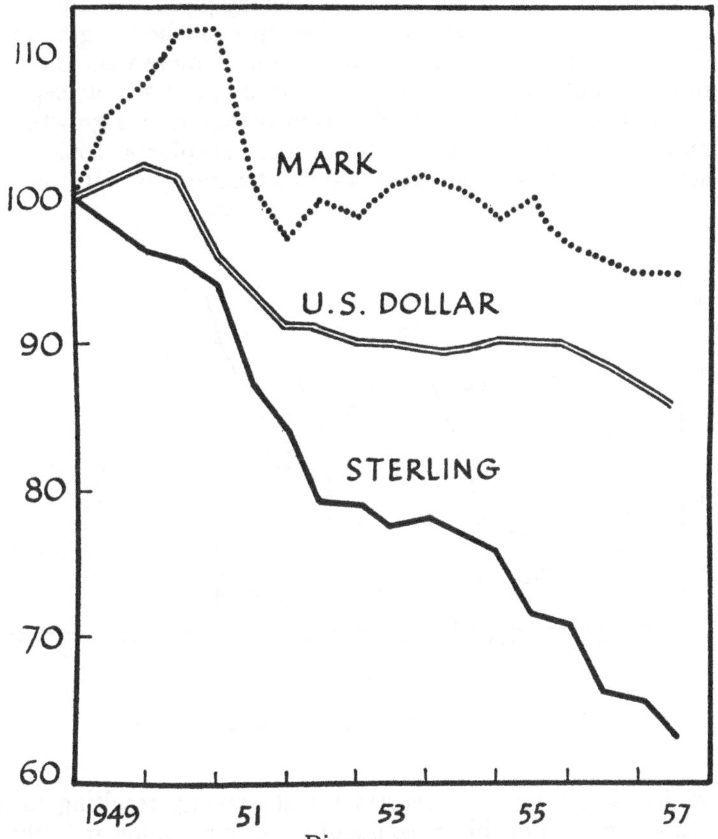

Diagram 12

Purchasing power of Pound, U.S. dollar and German mark as measured by retail prices. December 1948—100 in each case.

assets structure of the banks was highly liquid. In 1950 and early 1951, more than 40 per cent of deposits was at times represented by the traditional liquid assets alone, without taking Treasury deposit receipts into the calculation.

The second restraining influence was the maintenance of an over-all budget surplus. The underlying theory was that, since voluntary savings would not be forthcoming on a sufficient scale to finance the amount of investment taking place, they must be supplemented by compulsory saving through the budget. The Government therefore collected in taxation more than enough to cover, not only its ordinary expenditure, but also its capital expenditures 'below the line'. Given the enormous growth of public spending, unfortunately, such surpluses could be achieved only by means of a level of taxation so high that it

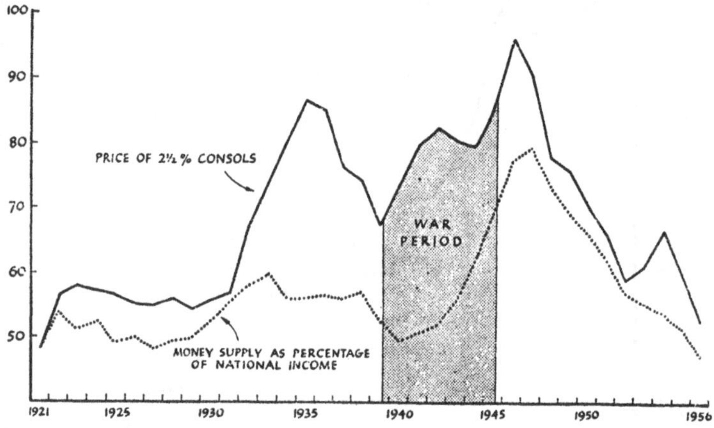

Diagram 13

Money stock and price of Consols, 1921 to 1956.

tended still further to depress private saving, resulting in a vicious spiral. For this reason, and because rationing and other wartime restraints on spending were being relaxed, the surpluses did no more than moderate the pace of inflation.

It should be noted that the rise in prices was not perceptibly quickened by the devaluation of sterling, in common with most other currencies, against the dollar in September 1949. What the ultimate effects on the price level would have been of the devaluation taken by itself we shall never know, for in June 1950 came the invasion of Korea. During the year following the devaluation, in any case, the retail price index rose by no more than 2 points. It was the boom in world commodity prices

MONEY STOCK AND GILT-EDGED

Year	Average Price of Consols	Money Supply as % of. Nat. Income
1921	48·0	48·3
2	56·5	53·9
3	58·0	51·2
4	57·0	52·4
5	56·4	49·1
6	55·0	49·8
7	54·8	48·1
8	55·9	49·2
9	54·3	49·7
1930	55·75	52·4
1	56·9	55·5
2	66·8	58·0
3	73·7	59·9
4	80·7	55·9
5	86·5	56·0
6	85·0	56·4
7	76·2	56·0
8	74·1	54·9
9	67·2	50·1
1940	73·5	47·5
1	79·9	48·9
2	82·5	50·4
3	80·6	54·4
4	79·6	60·8
5	85·6	68·6
6	96·3	77·0
7	90·6	79·0
8	78·0	72·3
9	75·9	69·0
1950	70·5	65·7
1	66·1	61·3
2	59·1	56·9
3	61·3	55·0
4	66·6	54·0
5	60·0	51·2
6	52·8	46·7
7	50·2	45·5
8	50·2	45·1
9	51·8	45·1
1960	46·1	44·3
1	40·3	42·7
2	41·8	41·9
3	44·8	41·6

CLEARING BANKS' NET DEPOSITS

Lloyds Bank Index, 1954—100, Adjusted for seasonal variations

	1955	1957	1959	1961	1963
January	101·6	97·3	103·6	110·7	117·9
February	102·2	96·9	102·9	111·5	118·2
March	101·0	96·9	104·1	111·8	119·7
April	101·0	96·6	103·7	113·2	118·7
May	100·2	97·9	103·4	113·1	119·6
*June	98·4	98·2	105·6	113·4	122·2
July	98·7	99·3	105·8	114·0	120·6
August	98·6	98·9	106·7	113·4	121·8
September	97·6	98·6	108·0	112·8	122·4
October	97·0	98·6	109·4	112·6	123·0
November	96·6	98·6	109·6	112·9	124·4
*December	95·9	99·8	108·9	114·0	125·2
	1956	**1958**	**1960**	**1962**	**1964**
January	96·9	99·9	110·2	113·8	125·0
February	96·4	100·1	110·2	113·9	125·2
March	95·9	100·1	109·5	115·1	127·1
April	95·9	100·8	109·5	114·2	127·1
May	96·0	100·2	109·6	114·8	127·6
*June	95·3	101·2	110·0	116·7	129·0
July	95·8	101·8	109·8	115·7	
August	96·1	101·2	110·3	116·0	
September	96·5	101·7	110·5	116·3	
October	96·7	101·9	110·0	116·8	
November	96·2	102·8	110·4	117·3	
*December	97·0	103·4	110·9	118·9	

* End-June and end-December throughout.

following the invasion of Korea which speeded up the pace of an inflation that would doubtless have continued in any event. In the first half of 1951, prices, wages, bank advances and bank deposits were all rising rapidly. So, paradoxically, were the gold reserves: for in the first instance the higher prices received by overseas sterling countries for their primary products helped to strengthen the balance of payments of the sterling area *vis-à-vis* the rest of the world. The reserves rose to a peak of $3,867 millions in June 1951, a level that has never since been regained. The sequel was catastrophic. With the United Kingdom replacing at boom prices the commodity stocks run down in the previous year, and with overseas sterling countries drawing heavily on the balances built up during the boom, no less than $2,205 millions of gold ran out in the brief period of ten months.

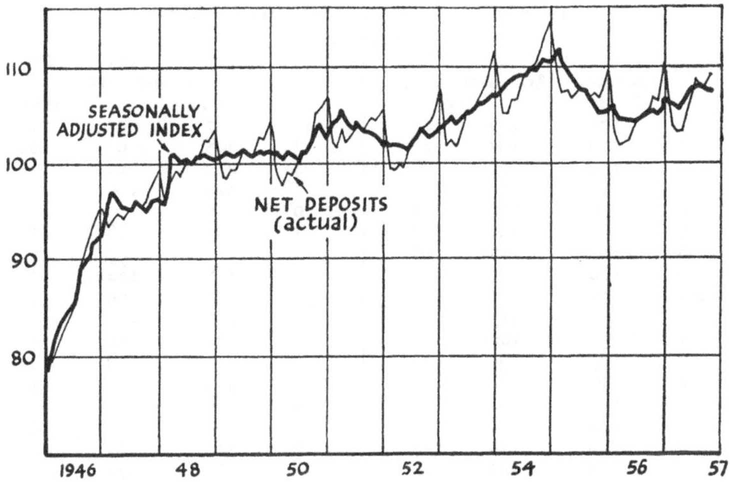

Diagram 14

Index of clearing bank net deposits, adjusted for seasonal variations, 1948—100.

The change of government thus took place with the worst of all the post-war external crises at its height. To some extent, the measures adopted followed the pattern of those used in the 1947 and 1949 crises: import cuts, a reduction in the tourist allowance, restrictions on hire purchase, revised instructions to the Capital Issues Committee, a letter to the banks tightening up the advances directives. What was new was the decision to revive the pre-1932 machinery of credit control. The ½ per cent money tap was closed. Bank Rate was raised from 2 to 2½ per cent, though advances against commercial bills and bonds were not to be made at that rate (not, as was traditional, at ½ per cent over Bank Rate), while a special rate of 2 per cent was fixed for advances against Treasury bills. In March 1952, with the gold outflow still continuing, Bank Rate was raised to 4 per cent. Meanwhile, and more important, the liquidity of the banks had been reduced by the funding of £1,000 millions of Treasury bills against 1¾ per cent stock of up to three years maturity. This had the effect of bringing down liquidity ratios to not so

ADVANCES AND NATIONAL INCOME

1922—100

	(1) National Income	(2) Advances	(2) as % of (1)		(1) National Income	(2) Advances	(2) as % of (1)
1922	100	100	23	1942	197	95	11
3	100	103	24	3	208	92	10
4	102	111	26	4	213	93	10
5	103	117	27	5	214	100	11
6	102	122	28	6	211	119	13
7	108	123	27	7	223	146	15
8	108	127	28	8	241	165	16
9	109	129	28	9	258	184	17
1930	103	121	28	1950	271	199	17
1	95	115	28	1	297	235	18
2	93	100	25	2	322	212	15
3	97	95	23	3	343	208	14
4	101	98	23	4	367	231	15
5	107	101	22	5	388	224	13
6	114	109	22	6	420	231	13
7	120	120	23	7	445	228	12
8	124	120	23	8	468	271	14
9	133	122	22	9	490	356	17
1940	157	110	16	1960	521	417	19
1	180	99	13	1	556	428	18
				2	579	456	18
				3	609	514	20

much over the conventional 30 per cent minimum. (See Diagram 17.)

By mid-1952, the crisis had been overcome; thereafter, the reserves climbed steadily upwards again, to cross the $3,000 million mark in the middle of 1954 – another temporary peak not regained until May 1958. The swing back from serious deficit to comfortable surplus in the balance of payments was due largely to more favourable terms of trade, and we cannot know what part the measures adopted by the United Kingdom may have played in promoting the relapse of world commodity prices from their Korean peak levels. What is certain is that for the first time since the war the pressure of excessive demand on the U.K. economy abated for a time. The official measures had a sobering effect on business expectations generally, while a short-lived depression in the textile industries contributed to the general slackening in demand. Wage rates continued to rise but, thanks to the fall in import prices, the cost of living index remained stable for a few months.

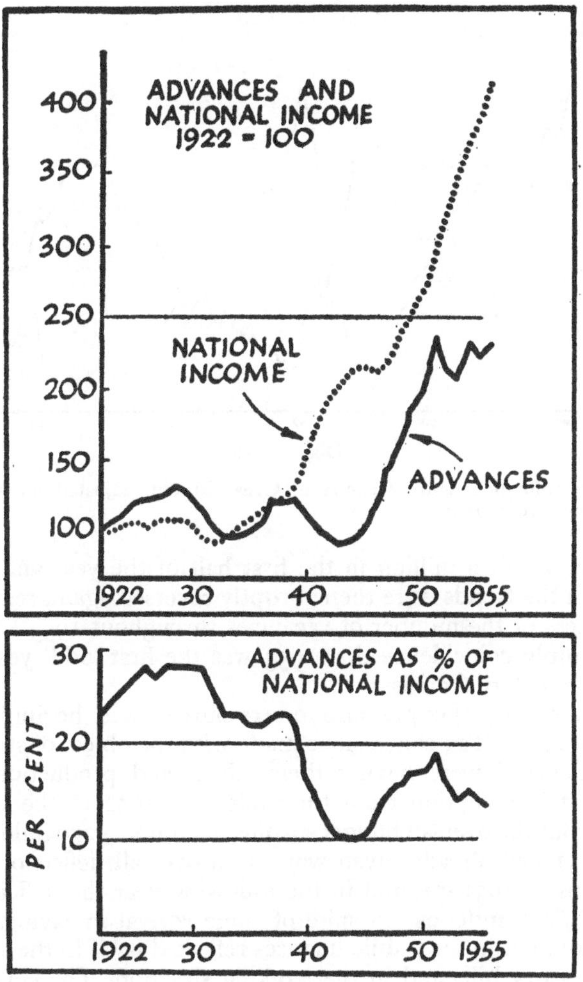

Diagram 15

For many years previously, unemployment had remained at extremely low levels, with far more vacancies on offer than workpeople seeking jobs. In 1952 the postion changed. With the number of vacancies falling, unemployment rose to a peak

M

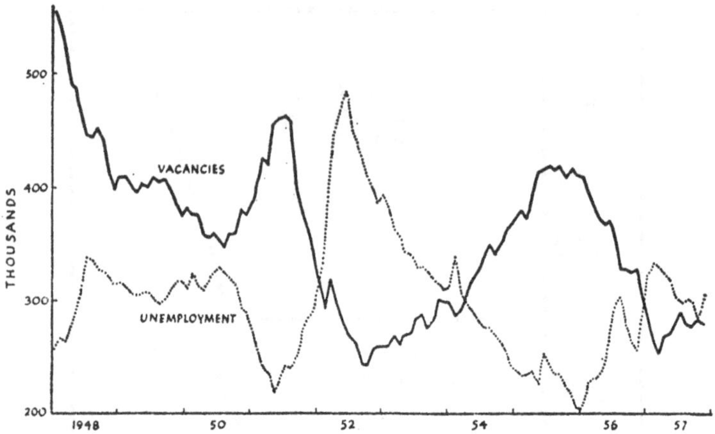

Diagram 16

Unemployment and vacancies in Great Britain, adjusted for seasonal variations, 1948–1957.

of nearly half a million in the first half of the year and, even though the trends were then abruptly reversed again, remained in excess of the number of vacancies throughout 1953.[1] It was not simply coincidence that 1953 was the first 'odd' year free from an external crisis.

Meanwhile, the pressure on resources was beginning to mount again. Tax concessions made with the object of stimulating demand were having their effect, and production rose without interruption from the middle of 1952 to the end of 1955. But the over-all budget surplus of around £250 millions in 1950–51 had already given way to an over-all deficit of £150 millions in 1951–52, and in the following year the deficit shot up to £436 millions. In spite of some revival in savings, this deterioration in the public finances reflected itself in the supply of Treasury bills and in the banking situation. The collective liquidity ratio in September 1952 was 38 per cent, almost as high as a year earlier, before the funding operation; in 1953 and 1954 the lowest ratios seen were 32·4 per cent and 32·9 per cent respectively. From the middle of 1952 to early 1955 bank depo-

1. See Diagram 16.

sits steadily expanded, the seasonally adjusted index rising by some 10 per cent over the period.

It is true that this expansion in the money supply did not quite keep pace with the growth of money incomes. But business confidence was high and, indeed, becoming exuberant. Notwithstanding the continued rise in the income velocity of bank deposits, therefore, the gilt-edged market experienced a minor boom in this period, the yield on Consols declining from 4·43 per cent in July 1952 to 3·64 per cent in November 1954.

In September 1953, Bank Rate had been reduced to 3½ per cent and the special rate for Treasury bill advances abandoned. As late as May 1954 the announcement of a further reduction to 3 per cent contributed to the boom atmosphere. Towards the end of the year there could no longer be any doubt that the economy was again in a highly inflationary state. The balance of payments with the dollar area became seriously adverse and a renewed loss of gold set in which lopped another $900 millions off the reserves by the end of 1955.

Apart from renewed restrictions on hire purchase, the counter measures taken on this occasion were of an exclusively monetary nature. Bank Rate was put up by ½ per cent in January 1955 and (as this was clearly unavailing) by a further full point to 4½ per cent a month later. At its higher level, moreover, Bank Rate was made 'effective' in the technical sense. Previously, the Treasury bill rate had been about 1½ per cent below Bank Rate; it now rose to within ½ per cent of the new and higher rate. The result was that over this period the return obtainable on Treasury bills rose by about 1 per cent more than that obtainable on deposit accounts with the clearing banks. To take advantage of this improved differential, industrial companies and other customers of the banks shifted their funds into Treasury bills on a substantial scale. Coming on top of the seasonal revenue inflow, this brought a sharp fall in the liquid assets of the banks; in March, the combined liquidity ratio dropped as low as 29·9 per cent and as late as June was no higher than 30·1 per cent.[1]

Throughout this half-year, therefore, considerations of liquidity were acting as a powerful deterrent to new bank lending.

1. See table over and Diagram 17.

LIQUIDITY RATIO, 11 CLEARING BANKS

	%	%	%	%	%	%	%
	1951*	1953	1955	1957	1959	1961	1963
Jan.	47·0	35·4	34·5	37·5	34·9	33·1	34·6
Feb.	44·0	33·1	31·3	33·6	32·3	31·1	31·6
Mar.	42·6	32·9	29·9	32·6	31·0	30·4	30·5
Apl.	43·6	32·4	30·5	32·6	31·2	32·0	30·5
May	41·8	33·6	30·5	32·9	30·9	31·5	30·7
†June	41·5	34·8	30·1	33·4	32·0	31·2	31·0
July	42·7	35·5	31·3	35·5	32·7	32·9	31·4
Aug.	42·1	36·8	32·0	35·3	32·9	32·9	31·3
Sept.	42·0	37·4	33·5	35·4	33·2	34·3	32·2
Oct.	41·9	36·6	33·8	36·2	34·4	35·0	32·3
Nov.	33·7	36·5	35·0	36·9	33·6	34·6	32·3
†Dec.	34·8	36·7	37·4	38·4	34·3	36·1	33·3
	1952*	1954	1956	1958	1960	1962	1964
Jan.	34·8	36·2	37·6	37·8	34·3	36·1	33·0
Feb.	32·1	33·2	34·2	35·2	32·1	33·2	29·9
Mar.	31·8	33·0	33·1	33·9	31·5	32·6	29·7
Apl.	31·6	33·1	33·4	33·1	31·4	32·7	30·5
May	32·9	32·9	33·2	32·4	31·6	32·6	29·6
†June	34·7	33·0	33·6	32·8	30·8	32·4	28·8
July	35·9	33·2	34·4	33·8	31·2	33·2	
Aug.	37·5	33·5	35·6	33·4	31·4	33·2	
Sept.	38·0	33·6	36·9	33·4	31·6	33·7	
Oct.	34·9	34·3	37·1	32·2	31·5	33·5	
Nov.	35·0	34·2	36·3	33·7	31·3	33·3	
†Dec.	36·0	34·3	37·4	34·6	32·6	35·9	

* Including T.D.R.s up to February 1952

† End-June and end-December throughout.

As is always the case, the banks had outstanding commitments to their borrowing customers, so that it was some months before the rise in advances could be checked. With the liquidity ratio at the irreducible minimum, however, the additional advances could be accommodated only by sales of investments. The banks' portfolios were in fact lightened by some £250 millions during these six months. Hence the expansion in advances did not mean a corresponding rise in deposits; on the contrary, the credit expansion in progress for nearly three years was reversed after February.

During the first half of 1955, in other words, monetary policy, for the first time in many years, was operating in the classical

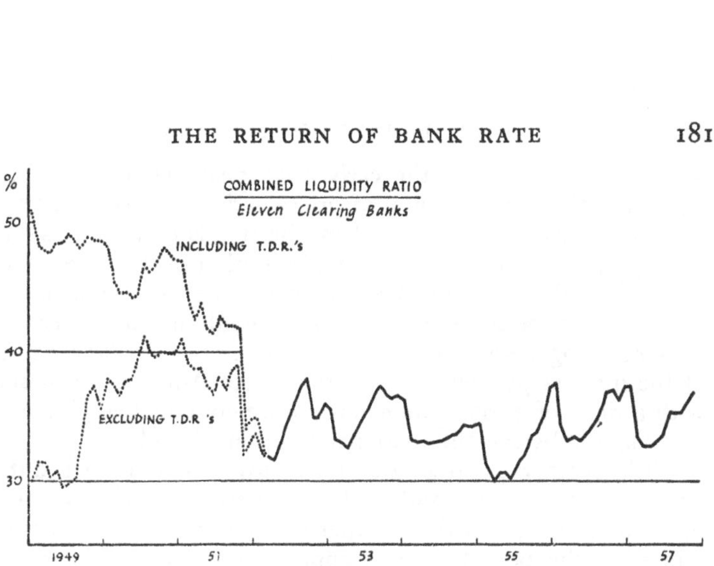

Diagram 17

fashion, with the authorities in full control of the situation. Unfortunately, they were in no position to sustain the pressure on bank liquidity. By the middle of the year it was clear that a marked expansion in the supply of Treasury bills could be expected in the coming months, to finance not only the normal seasonal deficit but also the requirements of the nationalized industries. (In the second half of the year the liquid assets of the banks in fact rose by £509 millions and the liquidity ratio in January 1956 was as high as 37·6 per cent.) It was against this background that in July 1955 the Chancellor took the unprecedented step of calling for 'a positive and significant reduction' in bank advances during the ensuing months.[1]

This action broke the boom in the industrial share markets but for some time had little apparent effect on the economy. 'At the beginning of 1956', as the Economic Survey observed, 'the United Kingdom economy was still in an inflationary condition.' Hence a fresh batch of restrictions was announced in the spring, even though the balance of payments was no longer in deficit.

Towards the end of the year, the disinflationary policy seemed to be making headway, though the picture was not entirely convincing. Clearing bank deposits (after falling by

1. See Appendix

some 7 per cent from the early 1955 peak) were expanding again and the upward spiral of prices and wages had not been completely arrested. Nevertheless, the trends of vacancies and unemployment reflected a steady diminution in the pressure of demand on the economy. Unfortunately, the Suez crisis intervened to reverse the rebuilding of the gold and dollar reserve earlier in progress and the year closed with a request for a waiver of the interest payment due on the North American loan and with a draft of $560 millions on the timely facilities placed at our disposal by the International Monetary Fund.

Little further progress was made towards a more healthy balance between demand and resources after the opening months of 1957, and the summer brought another speculative attack on the pound, due to apprehensions about the rising trend of wages combined with misapprehensions about the possibility of a change in the dollar-sterling rate.

The authorities therefore took fresh action, though not until the gold reserves had been pushed well below the $2,000 million mark. On September 19th, Bank Rate was raised from 5 to 7 per cent, the banks were asked to effect a further quantitative limitation of advances and the Chancellor gave an undertaking that investment expenditure in the public sector would be held down.[1]

* * *

Nearly six years after the unsheathing of the Bank Rate weapon, then, the erosion of the purchasing power of the pound had not manifestly been stopped and we were passing through yet another external crisis. In retrospect, indeed, the twelve years following the war appear as a period of almost uninterrupted inflation without precedent in peacetime. In no single one of those twelve years was the purchasing power of the pound as high at the end as at the beginning. (See chart on p. 171). Moreover, there had been an external crisis of one kind or another in every 'odd' year from 1947 onwards, with the sole exception of 1953. Neither the change of government nor the 'unfreezing' of Bank Rate in 1951 noticeably affected the major trends in the monetary field. What had gone wrong?

1. See Appendix.

Whatever view may be taken about the reasons for inflation, it is clear that an upper limit must exist to the stream of income-generating expenditures that can be sustained without a rise in prices. To stop an inflation, therefore, means to prevent the flow of incomes from rising above this critical level. In that endeavour, a great variety of official actions, and not simply actions in the monetary field, can play their part. So far as monetary policies are concerned, however, we have to remember that a given flow of incomes can be generated either by a relatively large stock of money turning over relatively slowly, or by a smaller money stock turning over more rapidly. In principle, therefore, monetary policies designed to counter inflation can operate either on the size of the money stock, or upon its velocity of circulation, or upon both at the same time.

Nevertheless, there are strong grounds for arguing that limitation of the money stock is fundamental. This is not just for the simple reason that persons and companies will tend to spend more freely if they have ample balances in the bank than if they have not. More important, the size of the money stock has a direct bearing upon the long-term rate of interest: if the supply of liquid assets is reduced, long-term rates of interest will tend to rise, encouraging the postponement of expenditure. Admittedly, that will not be the only effect. If the economy becomes less liquid, some balances formerly left idle may well be tempted into active use. But that merely emphasizes how much slack there must have been in the first place and points the need to carry the contraction further. As the Macmillan Committee pointed out, 'whilst a buoyant and optimistic market for investment and enterprise may contrive for a time to carry on the same volume of business with a diminished supply of credit, there are definite limitations to the possibilities of this.'

Looking back, it seems clear that one of the chief reasons for the failure of monetary policy in these years lay in the failure to reduce bank deposits. It might seem plausible to argue that after 1951 velocity factors had been the more important, as deposits had not been greatly increased and the inflation had been financed mainly by a cumulative rise in their rate of turnover. That would be absurdly superficial. To say that velocity has risen is simply to state that the rate of growth of the money stock has been less than the rate of growth of incomes. It can import no judgment whatever on the significant issue: whether the money stock at the outset was not too large, so that deposits ought rather to have been reduced than allowed to increase at all.

The mere fact that inflation continued is sufficient proof that the money stock had been excessive, but two more specific reasons can be advanced to show why a contraction was necessary. The first is that, although the income velocity of deposits had been rising since 1947, the money stock in 1951 was still much higher in relation to national income than in the years before the war.[1] The second reason is that over the period as a whole the gold and dollar reserves had on balance fallen.

It is true that the supply of credit has not been unaffected by changes in the reserves. Any influx of gold has been financed, automatically and as a matter of course, by means of Treasury bills and an expansion of bank deposits, without reference to the requirements of the monetary situation as a whole. On the other hand, a loss of gold has tended, just as automatically, to exert some influence in the opposite direction. Bank deposits were in fact falling, under the influence of heavy gold losses, at the time the change of policy took place; but whereas the gold reserves fell by nearly £800 millions between June 1951 and April 1952, net clearing bank deposits (allowing for seasonal variations) contracted by less than £100 millions over those ten months. (See Table below.)

	Changes in gold reserve £m	Changes in adjusted net deposits* £m
June 1951 to April 1952	−787	−88
April 1952 to Feb. 1955	+364	+564
Feb. 1955 to July 1956	−99	−407
July 1956 to Sept. 1957	−198	+157
Sept. 1957 to July 1958	+440	+223

* As calculated for Lloyds Bank's seasonally adjusted index of deposits.

1. See Diagram 13.

In the succeeding years, with the reserves recovering, the expansion in net deposits between April 1952 and February 1955 exceeded the influx of gold by £200 millions. On the other hand, if the period from February 1955 to July 1958 is taken as a whole, a further influx of nearly £150 millions of gold was accompanied by a slight fall, on balance, in net deposits (though even in this phase there was little reflection, in the trend of deposits, of the gold losses of the second half of 1956 and the summer of 1957).

Except in 1955 and early 1956 (when deposits were reduced by sales of investments and the impact of the 'credit squeeze' on advances), powerful forces were clearly at work to prevent the reduction in deposits, and in the supply of Treasury bills, that might have been expected to result from pressure on the exchange reserves and the increase in the currency circulation. The nature of those forces cannot be in doubt; they are connected with the unbroken series of over-all deficits in the national finances. It is true that the deficits have been financed only to a relatively small extent by the creation of additional bank credit.[1] But it has already been argued that what the situation demanded was a contraction in the money supply.

Obviously, the persistent over-all deficit has been pulling in the contrary direction; but had the funding of deposits been all along the primary objective, the deficit would not have been an insuperable obstacle. The key period in this connection is 1954. Conditions in that year followed the classical pattern of an inflationary boom, with business confidence buoyant the economy at full stretch, costs and prices tending upwards. The authorities undoubtedly had it within their power to fund deposits at that time had they been so disposed; for, in spite of the rising income velocity of deposits, gilt-edged were passing through a minor boom which did not culminate until the final weeks of the year. So far from pursuing an active funding policy, in other words, the authorities did not even increase the supply of long-term securities commensurately with the demand

1. Over the six calendar years 1952 to 1957 inclusive, the net deposits of the clearing banks rose by nearly £500 millions, or 8 per cent, notwithstanding a fall of some £100 millions in advances and commercial bills and a rise of over £550 millions in the currency circulation.

for them. Hence the expansion of bank deposits in progress from the middle of 1952 continued until early 1955.

If at that time the authorities had been draining off bank deposits by sales of securities, driving up the long-term interest rate instead of allowing it to decline, much subsequent history might have been different. In particular, action on these lines might have helped to moderate the increase in velocity that many regard as the central difficulty. Instead, attempts were made to slow down velocity by more direct methods: the control of hire purchase, more stringent control of capital issues, successive tightenings of the advances squeeze.

Measures of this kind seek to influence the pattern of economic activity by decisions taken at the centre, and at the cost of interference with freedom of contract. Consequently, they run counter to the basic philosophy of a free price system and have little affinity with monetary policy proper, whose great recommendation, in the eyes of some people, is its impartial and all-pervasive character. That would matter less if such measures promised to be really effective. In fact, they treat symptoms and not underlying causes.

Confronted by an inflationary rise in velocity, the authorities in effect chose to leave an excessive money supply in existence while trying to prevent the surplus money from finding its way into active use. This is equivalent to placing little dams in the path of a swollen stream. If people in general have plenty of money one cannot expect to achieve a great deal by the control of borrowing – still less by the restriction of borrowing through particular channels: lenders and borrowers can be relied upon to carve out new channels between themselves, as witness the attraction of deposits from the public by the hire purchase finance companies.

It is true that in its early stages the 'credit squeeze' of 1955 helped to reduce the liquidity of the economy, since the contraction in total advances helped to sustain the contraction in deposits started by the heavy sales of bank investments earlier in the year. But an important feature of the squeeze was its selective character. There is no evidence that industries whose bank accommodation was most severely curtailed found themselves compelled on that account to reduce their activities; on the contrary they seem, in one way or another, to have succeeded in financing a substantial increase in money turnover. In any event, a situation like that from the middle of 1956 to the middle of 1958, in which the banks were operating a selective squeeze on advances with the trend of deposits steadily rising, has no logic whatever.

It is clear that the effective way to operate upon velocity is to influence the expectations of the public. Velocity will fall when it ceases to be assumed that the trend of prices will always be upwards, that higher costs can always be passed on to the consumer, that easy profits can always be made with the use of borrowed money. In short, the disposition to hold money will increase if money seems likely to be worth holding. Moreover, if investors have some assurance of repayment in money of the same value as that invested, funds will flow more readily into fixed securities and the authorities will be able to make headway with the underlying task of funding floating debt and reducing the money supply. The problem is to break the vicious circle.

CHAPTER XVII

POSTSCRIPT: FROM CRISIS TO CRISIS

ON the announcement of Mr. Thorneycroft's measures in September 1957 the gold drain ceased abruptly. During 1958 it was therefore possible to make several successive reductions in Bank Rate without stemming the sustained recovery in the exchange reserves which carried them well over the $3,000 billions mark in the latter part of the year. For some months the cost of living continued to rise but by mid-year the upward movement had exhausted itself. In June the index settled at the level of 110 which was not to be exceeded for a full two years and so marked the beginning of the so-called 'price plateau' – the first real respite from inflation since the beginning of the war.

It must remain a matter of controversy how far these results were attributable to any technical results of the crisis measures and how far to the government's professed determination to halt inflation, even if necessary at the cost of something more than the usual minimal unemployment and of possible unpleasantness on the wages front. By July 1958, in any event, it was clear that the internal and external dangers to the pound had been overcome, and the restrictions on bank advances (originally imposed for twelve months) were lifted.

From the monetary viewpoint, the chief effect on the banks of the 'liberation' of July 1958 was to correct the distortion of their assets structure resulting from nearly twenty years of directives. Advances were abnormally low, in relation both to deposits and to current price and income levels,[1] at under £2,000 millions; bond portfolios were as abnormally high, at

1. See table on page 176.

appreciably more than that figure. With the release of the pent-up demand for bank accommodation, something more like the pre-war pattern of assets was restored within three years. By mid-1961 advances had almost doubled, the ratio of advances to deposits rising from 30·3 per cent in August to 47·2 per cent in July 1961. To accommodate the additional advances the bond portfolios were more than halved, with a decline in the investments ratio from 33·4 per cent to 13·9 per cent over the same period. At that level, indeed, it was the investments ratio which had now fallen abnormally low by pre-war standards.

CLEARING BANKS: MAIN ITEMS

	August 1958 £m	*August* 1961 £m	*Change* £m
Assets			
Liquid assets	2,199	2,450	+251
Special deposits ..	Nil	185	+185
Investments	2,199	1,047	−1,152
Advances	1,993	3,446	+1,453
Deposits			
Gross	6,576	7,437	+861
Net	6,312	7,079	+767
Ratios	%	%	
Liquidity ratio ..	33·4	32·9	
Investment ratio ..	33·4	14·1	
Advances ratio ..	30·3	46·3	

Long before this process was completed, however, inflationary trends had been allowed to reassert themselves and the country was to find itself in the throes of yet another crisis fully as severe as that of 1957. The watershed between the two crises was probably the middle of 1959. At that point of time the economic position of the country could have been described almost in glowing terms. For the first time since the war the cost of living had been stable for a full twelve months. The previous year had brought a bumper surplus of well over £300 millions in the balance of payments. The exchange reserves were at their highest level for many years. Production had been expanding rapidly since the beginning of the year, establishing new records every month, and productivity was also on the upgrade. Unemployment was coming down from the (seasonally adjusted) peak of just over 2½ per cent at the turn of the year but had not yet fallen below the 2 per cent level which is the infallible danger signal. Finally, the surplus of liquid assets of the early post-war years had gradually been eliminated by the process of inflation itself; the stock of money was no longer manifestly excessive. Prosperity without inflation, in fact. The task of the authorities was merely to consolidate the gains which had been achieved.

By the turn of the year signs of renewed strain were already apparent and the emphasis in official policy was shifted from stimulation to restraint of the economy. In January 1960 Bank Rate was raised to 5 per cent and a few weeks later the authorities allowed the prices of short-term bonds to fall, a move designed, it was supposed, to help restrain bank advances by penalizing the liquidation of investments.

In the spring of 1960, therefore, the great question was whether the Budget would at least fit in with this pattern of restraining action. After a brief respite, due no doubt to Mr. Thorneycroft's gallant stand, government expenditure was again rising and the pre-budget estimates indicated a further increase of as much as 8 per cent. Clearly, some pretty austere budgeting would be needed simply to prevent the public finances from adding to other sources of inflationary pressure, quite apart from any question of using the budget as a stablizing instrument. The nettle was not grasped. The budget actually presented for 1960/61 envisaged an over-all deficit ('borrowing requirement') a few millions *larger* than in the previous financial year, at £318 millions, and in the event the actual deficit for the year was not far short of £400 millions. In terms of calendar years (see table) the above-line surplus in 1960 was reduced by more than £250 millions and the over-all deficit increased by more than £175 millions.

Against this fiscal background the boom – inevitably – continued. The balance of payments became ever worse, with a deficit of nearly £250 millions in the second half of the year; and in the final months retail prices began to rise again after more than two years of stability. For the time being, however,

Calendar years £ millions	*Ordinary revenue*	*Ordinary expenditure*	*Above-line surplus*	*Net below-line expenditure*	*Over-all deficit*
1957	5,306	4,876	430	732	302
8	5,425	5,054	371	614	243
9	5,636	5,208	428	691	263
60	5,794	5,619	175	615	440
61	6,363	6,116	247	540	293
Changes on year:					
1958	+119	+178	−59	−118	−59
9	+211	+154	+57	+77	+20
60	+158	+411	−253	−76	+177
61	+569	+497	+72	−75	−147

the pressure on the exchange reserves that was otherwise to be expected was staved off by a large-scale inflow of short-term funds. This was the result partly of relatively attractive short-term rates[1] but also of some international concern about the position of the dollar.

A wave of distrust affecting the whole structure of exchange rates was set up by the belated and inadequate revaluation of the German currency in early 1961. And it was the massive exodus from sterling prompted by this fresh uncertainty which precipitated the crisis and brought the realities of our situation into the open. Even the published figures of the gold and exchange reserves showed a fall of nearly £300 millions between January and July, notwithstanding supporting purchases of sterling by European central banks (under the so-called Basle Agreement) to the tune at one time of £325 millions.

The budget of April 1961 was on lines which twelve months earlier might have averted a great deal of trouble. Not only did the estimates provide for the virtual elimination of the over-all deficit (in spite of a further rise in expenditure) but provision was made for the further reinforcement of the revenue if need be through a surcharge of up to 10 per cent in customs and excise duties. The maximum surcharge was in fact imposed towards the end of July when the Chancellor announced a batch of crisis measures, including the much-discussed 'pay pause'.

1. After being raised to 6 per cent in June, Bank Rate was reduced in two steps to 5 per cent before the year ended.

In the monetary sphere, Bank Rate was raised from 5 to 7 per cent, there was a further call for special deposits[1] and the banks were asked to limit the growth of their advances, being particularly severe 'towards advances for purposes of personal consumption, including hire purchase, and for speculative building, property development and other speculative purposes'. Freedom from directives, in other words, had lasted exactly three years and the system of special deposits (in which 3 per cent of the banks' deposit resources were now impounded) had become not an alternative to directives but superimposed upon them.

* * *

The 1957 and 1961 crises arose out of remarkably similar situations; in each case, for example, unemployment had fallen below 1½ per cent and the proportion of Government expenditure covered from revenue well below 95 per cent, prices and costs were rising sharply and exports making little headway. Similarly, the course of events after the 1963 crisis ran closely parallel to those after the 1957 crisis. The upsurge in prices and costs was moderated. Industrial production dipped slightly in the final months of 1961, the index falling back from 116 to 113, and unemployment rose to end the year at 1·7 per cent. It continued rising in 1962, to cross the 2 per cent mark in June; but the level of production was also rising and as early as May the pre-crisis peak level had been regained. Indeed, the opening weeks of 1962 saw the beginnings of a sustained upswing which raised the index to a new record level of 126 by early 1964.

This trend was, however, interrupted and for a time disguised by the effects of the exceptionally severe winter of 1962–3, with the result that unemployment rose sharply over the turn of the year. Following on incentives previously announced,[2] a further

1. See Appendix.

2. In October 1962, release of post-war credits, removal of restraints on bank lending and prospective increase in public investment; in November, increased investment allowances and a cut in purchase tax on cars; in December, release of remaining Special Deposits; in January, further, cuts in purchase tax, a reduction in Bank Rate from 4½ to 4 per cent and substantial increases in unemployment, sickness and other social benefits.

stimulus to expansion was provided in April 1963 by substantial tax concessions in a budget which envisaged an over-all deficit of nearly £700 millions.

The medicine, as has been seen, was effective and the economic pattern of 1963 was very similar to that of 1959, with production rising to new record levels, productivity rising even faster, wage costs per unit of output tending to fall and – most important of all – with exports showing renewed expansion and the balance of payments in surplus.

By the early months of 1964 the economy was manifestly approaching full stretch, with unemployment below the critical 2 per cent level and tending lower. The need to moderate expansion was recognised in February by an increase in Bank Rate from 4 to 5 per cent and it was generally expected that the budget would impose significant restraints on demand. About £100 millions of purchasing power was indeed drained off by increased taxes on tobacco and alcohol; but the estimates nevertheless provided for an over-all deficit, in this tight situation, about half as large again as that which had helped to absorb all the slack in the economy over the previous twelve months. If a relapse is avoided into the sort of conditions which in the past have produced crises it is not, clearly, fiscal policy that we shall have to thank.

APPENDIX

From Directives to Directives plus Special Deposits

Restrictions upon the freedom of the banks to conduct their lending operations in accordance with normal banking considerations were continuously in operation from the outbreak of war in 1939 until July 1958.

At the outset, the requests took a qualitative form, the banks being requested to restrict advances to purposes regarded as essential to the war effort and therefore to refrain from certain types of lending, such as advances for speculative purposes (notably the buying or holding of Stock Exchange securities or the acquisition of commodity stocks). In May 1945, the type of activities to be viewed with favour were defined afresh to include the promotion of exports (or saving of imports), industrial re-equipment and certain other projects. It was not until the crisis of 1951 that the banks were expected actively to discourage the production of 'inessential' goods for the home market.

The directives took a new turn when in July 1955 the banks were asked, in addition to observing the selective requests already in operation, to achieve 'a positive and significant reduction in their advances' during the ensuing months. A further quantitative request was issued in September 1957, the then Chancellor stating the general situation required that advances in the ensuing twelve months should be held at the average for the preceding twelve months (excluding medium-term advances guaranteed by the Export Credits Guarantee Department).

Before the expiry of this twelve-month period, i.e., in early July 1958, the Chancellor announced that he had decided he 'need not ask the banks to restrict the total level of their advances to any given figure after the end of July' and that some gradual relaxation between then and September was justified. As to the future,

> 'it would clearly be wise to await the recommendations of the Radcliffe Committee before considering any permanent changes in the methods of influencing the volume of bank lending. I regard it as essential, however, that in the interim period some provisional method should be at hand to reinforce the existing machinery of interest rates and open market operations if it should again prove necessary to restrain an increase of total bank advances.
>
> Both the Bank of England and the banking organizations have repeatedly impressed upon H.M. Government that the method of 'official requests' made to the banks several times in recent years to restrict total advances, although it has proved efficacious for short periods, hampers the efficient working of the banking system and is thus damaging both to the banks and to the public interest if carried on for too long or too frequently renewed.
>
> I accept this view and I should therefore be grateful if the Bank of England would between now and the end of July prepare an alternative scheme which could, if necessary, be introduced as a temporary measure pending the Radcliffe Committee's report.'

Replying to the Chancellor, the Governor gave the following broad outline of the new special deposits scheme:

> 'When it appeared necessary, in support of other monetary measures, to restrict the liquidity of the banking system and thus the ability of the banks to extend credit, the Bank of England would call for special deposits to be made with them by the banks. Such deposits would carry interest based on the current Treasury Bill rate. They would not qualify for inclusion in the banks' liquid assets. There would be provision for partial release by agreement with the Bank of England when justified by special considerations.
>
> The banks would continue to maintain their usual minimum ratios between liquid assets and total deposits.

Calls would be made on each group of banks separately, the amount being related to the total gross deposits of each group at a specified date with monthly adjustments to take account of variations in the deposits of each bank. The ratio of a call to total deposits would not necessarily be the same for each group.

Initially, the scheme is being discussed with the Clearing and Scottish Banks, but it might later be more widely applied in the light of experience. The scheme would serve to reinforce the existing monetary instruments and would be employed as a general control of credit in the same way and after the same sort of consideration as Bank Rate.'

In 1960 and 1961, the clearing banks were called upon, as shown below, to provide Special Deposits totalling 3 per cent of their deposits. (On each occasion the Scottish banks were also called upon to the extent of half the percentage applied to the clearing banks):

Date of call	*For payment by:*	*Amount (as % of deposits)* %	*Liquidity ratio at time of call* %
1960			
April 28	June 15	1	31·4
June 23	July 20	½	31·4
1961			
July 25	Aug. 17	½	32·9
	Aug. 16	½	
	Sep. 20	½	

July 1961, when the third call was announced, saw the peak of the upsurge in advances, with an advances ratio for the clearing banks of 47·2 per cent. In the succeeding months advances declined sharply and by the end of the year the advances ratio had fallen back to 42 per cent.

During 1962 the crisis measures were reversed in a series of steps, with release of the Special Deposits in three equal stages announced in June, September and November. In early October the 1961 requests for restraint in particular fields of lending were withdrawn but the Governor expressed confidence that the banks 'would continue to give priority where necessary, and encouragement always, to activities which promoted exports and overseas earnings', while asking them 'in so far as it is within their power to give special consideration to the promotion of business in those areas of the country where resources are not being used to full capacity.'

With the economy making rapid headway, advances rose sharply during the first half of 1963, reaching nearly £4,000 millions in August with a ratio to deposits of 50 per cent. Although advances then levelled off for a time, the banks' liquidity ratios in the latter part of the year were on the low side and in October it was indicated that for the time being 28 per cent, instead of the conventional 30 per cent., would be an acceptable minimum (see page 89). Bank Rate was raised to 5 per cent in February 1964.

INDEX